CONTENTS

BREAKFAST CHAFFLE RECIPES

Chili Chaffle

Servings: 4
Cooking Time: 7–9 Minutes
Ingredients:

- Batter
- 4 eggs
- ½ cup grated parmesan cheese
- 1½ cups grated yellow cheddar cheese
- 1 hot red chili pepper
- Salt and pepper to taste
- ½ teaspoon dried garlic powder
- 1 teaspoon dried basil
- 2 tablespoons almond flour
- Other
- 2 tablespoons olive oil for brushing the waffle maker

Directions:

1. Preheat the waffle maker.
2. Crack the eggs into a bowl and add the grated parmesan and cheddar cheese.
3. Mix until just combined and add the chopped chili pepper. Season with salt and pepper, dried garlic powder and dried basil. Stir in the almond flour.
4. Mix until everything is combined.
5. Brush the heated waffle maker with olive oil and add a few tablespoons of the batter.
6. Close the lid and cook for about 7–8 minutes depending on your waffle maker.

Nutrition Info: Per Serving Calories 367, fat 30.4 g, carbs 3.1 g, sugar 0.7 g, Protein 21.5 g, sodium 469 mg

Crispy Chaffles With Egg & Asparagus

Servings: 1
Cooking Time: 10 Minutes
Ingredients:

- 1 egg
- 1/4 cup cheddar cheese
- 2 tbsps. almond flour
- ½ tsp. baking powder
- TOPPING
- 1 egg
- 4-5 stalks asparagus
- 1 tsp avocado oil

Directions:

1. Preheat waffle maker to medium-high heat.
2. Whisk together egg, mozzarella cheese, almond flour, and baking powder
3. Pour chaffles mixture into the center of the waffle iron. Close the waffle maker and let cook for 3-5 minutes or until waffle is golden brown and set.
4. Remove chaffles from the waffle maker and serve.

5. Meanwhile, heat oil in a nonstick pan.
6. Once the pan is hot, fry asparagus for about 4-5 minutes until golden brown.
7. Poach the egg in boil water for about 2-3 minutes.
8. Once chaffles are cooked, remove from the maker.
9. Serve chaffles with the poached egg and asparagus.

Nutrition Info: Per Serving: Protein: 26% 85 kcal Fat: 69% 226 kcal Carbohydrates: 5% 16 kcal

Delicious Raspberriestaco Chaffles

Servings: 1
Cooking Time: 15 Minutes

Ingredients:

- 1 egg white
- 1/4 cup jack cheese, shredded
- 1/4 cup cheddar cheese, shredded
- 1 tsp coconut flour
- 1/4 tsp baking powder
- 1/2 tsp stevia
- For Topping
- 4 oz. raspberries
- 2 tbsps. coconut flour
- 2 oz. unsweetened raspberry sauce

Directions:

1. Switch on yourround Waffle Maker and grease it with cooking spray once it is hot.
2. Mix together all chaffle ingredients in a bowl and combine with a fork.
3. Pour chaffle batter in a preheated maker and close the lid.
4. Roll the taco chaffle around using a kitchen roller, set it aside and allow it to set for a few minutes.
5. Once the taco chaffle is set, remove from the roller.
6. Dip raspberries in sauce and arrange on taco chaffle.
7. Drizzle coconut flour on top.
8. Enjoy raspberries taco chaffle with keto coffee.

Nutrition Info: Per Serving: Protein: 28% 77 kcal Fat: 69% 187 kcal Carbohydrates: 3% 8 kcal

Cajun & Feeta Chaffles

Servings: 1
Cooking Time: 10 Minutes

Ingredients:

- 1 egg white
- 1/4 cup shredded mozzarella cheese
- 2 tbsps. almond flour
- 1 tsp Cajun Seasoning
- FOR SERVING
- 1 egg
- 4 oz. feta cheese
- 1 tomato, sliced

Directions:

1. Whisk together egg, cheese, and seasoning in a bowl.
2. Switch on and grease waffle maker with cooking spray.
3. Pour batter in a preheated waffle maker.
4. Cook chaffles for about 2-3 minutes until the chaffle is cooked through.
5. Meanwhile, fry the egg in a non-stick pan for about 1-2 minutes.
6. For serving set fried egg on chaffles with feta cheese and tomatoes slice.

Nutrition Info: Per Serving: Protein: 28% 119 kcal Fat: 64% 270 kcal Carbohydrates: 7% 31 kcal

Mini Breakfast Chaffles

Servings: 3
Cooking Time: 15 Minutes

Ingredients:

- 6 tsp coconut flour
- 1 tsp stevia
- 1/4 tsp baking powder
- 2 eggs
- 3 oz. cream cheese
- 1/2. tsp vanilla extract
- Topping
- 1 egg
- 6 slice bacon
- 2 oz. Raspberries for topping
- 2 oz. Blueberries for topping
- 2 oz. Strawberries for topping

Directions:

1. Heat up your square waffle maker and grease with cooking spray.
2. Mix together coconut flour, stevia, egg, baking powder, cheese and vanilla in mixing bowl.
3. Pour ½ of chaffles mixture in a waffle maker.
4. Close the lid and cook the chaffles for about 3-5 minutes.
5. Meanwhile, fry bacon slices in pan on medium heat for about 2-3 minutes until cooked and transfer themto plate.
6. In the same pan, fry eggs one by one in the leftover grease of bacon.
7. Once chaffles are cooked, carefully transfer them to plate.
8. Serve with fried eggs and bacon slice and berries on top.
9. Enjoy!

Nutrition Info: Per Serving: Protein: 16% 75 kcal Fat: 75% 346 kcal Carbohydrates: 9% 41 kcal

Crispy Chaffles With Sausage

Servings: 2
Cooking Time: 10 Minutes

Ingredients:

- 1/2 cup cheddar cheese
- 1/2 tsp. baking powder

- 1/4 cup egg whites
- 2 tsp. pumpkin spice
- 1 egg, whole
- 2 chicken sausage
- 2 slice bacon
- salt and pepper to taste
- 1 tsp. avocado oil

Directions:

1. Mix together all ingredients in a bowl.
2. Allow batter to sit while waffle iron warms.
3. Spray waffle iron with nonstick spray.
4. Pour batter in the waffle maker and cook according to the directions of the manufacturer.
5. Meanwhile, heat oil in a pan and fry the egg, according to your choice and transfer it toa plate.
6. In the same pan, fry bacon slice and sausage on medium heat for about 2-3 minutes until cooked.
7. Once chaffles are cooked thoroughly, remove them from the maker.
8. Serve with fried egg, bacon slice, sausages and enjoy!

Nutrition Info: Per Serving: Protein: 22% 86 kcal Fat: 74% 286 kcal Carbohydrates: 3% 12 kcal

Chaffles Breakfast Bowl

Servings: 2
Cooking Time: 5 Minutes

Ingredients:

- 1 egg
- 1/2 cup cheddar cheese shredded
- pinch of Italian seasoning
- 1 tbsp. pizza sauce
- TOPPING
- 1/2 avocado sliced
- 2 eggs boiled
- 1 tomato, halves
- 4 oz. fresh spinach leaves

Directions:

1. Preheat yourwaffle maker and grease with cooking spray.
2. Crack an egg in a small bowl and beat with Italian seasoning and pizza sauce.
3. Add shredded cheese to the egg and spices mixture.
4. Pour 1 tbsp. shredded cheese in a waffle maker and cook for 30 sec.
5. Pour Chaffles batter inthe waffle maker and close the lid.
6. Cook chaffles for about 4 minutes until crispy and brown.
7. Carefully remove chaffles from the maker.
8. Serve on the bed of spinach with boil egg, avocado slice, and tomatoes.
9. Enjoy!

Nutrition Info: Per Serving: Protein: 23% 77 kcal Fat: 66% 222 kcal Carbohydrates: 11% 39 kcal

Avocado Chaffle Toast

Servings: 3
Cooking Time: 10 Minutes
Ingredients:

- 4 tbsps. avocado mash
- 1/2 tsp lemon juice
- 1/8 tsp salt
- 1/8 tsp black pepper
- 2 eggs
- 1/2 cup shredded cheese
- For serving
- 3 eggs
- ½ avocado thinly sliced
- 1 tomato, sliced

Directions:

1. Mash avocado mash with lemon juice, salt, and black pepper in mixing bowl, until well combined.
2. In a small bowl beat egg and pour eggs in avocado mixture and mix well.
3. Switch on Waffle Maker to pre-heat.
4. Pour 1/8 of shredded cheese in a waffle maker and then pour ½ of egg and avocado mixture and then 1/8 shredded cheese.
5. Close the lid and cook chaffles for about 3 - 4 minutes.
6. Repeat with the remaining mixture.
7. Meanwhile,fry eggs in a pan for about 1-2 minutes.
8. For serving, arrange fried egg on chaffle toast with avocado slice and tomatoes.
9. Sprinkle salt and pepper on top and enjoy!

Nutrition Info: Per Serving: Protein: 26% 66 kcal Fat: 67% 169 kcal Carbohydrates: 6% 15 kcal

Simple Savory Chaffle

Servings: 4
Cooking Time: 7–9 Minutes
Ingredients:

- Batter
- 4 eggs
- 1 cup grated mozzarella cheese
- 1 cup grated provolone cheese
- ½ cup almond flour
- 2 tablespoons coconut flour
- 2½ teaspoons baking powder
- Salt and pepper to taste
- Other
- 2 tablespoons butter to brush the waffle maker

Directions:

1. Preheat the waffle maker.
2. Add the grated mozzarella and provolone cheese to a bowl and mix.
3. Add the almond and coconut flour and baking powder and season with salt and pepper.

4. Mix with a wire whisk and crack in the eggs.
5. Stir everything together until batter forms.
6. Brush the heated waffle maker with butter and add a few tablespoons of the batter.
7. Close the lid and cook for about 7–8 minutes depending on your waffle maker.
8. Serve and enjoy.

Nutrition Info: Per Serving Calories 352, fat 27.2 g, carbs 8.3 g, sugar 0.5 g, Protein 19.5 g, sodium 442 mg

Scrambled Eggs On A Spring Onion Chaffle

Servings: 4
Cooking Time: 7–9 Minutes

Ingredients:

- Batter
- 4 eggs
- 2 cups grated mozzarella cheese
- 2 spring onions, finely chopped
- Salt and pepper to taste
- ½ teaspoon dried garlic powder
- 2 tablespoons almond flour
- 2 tablespoons coconut flour
- Other
- 2 tablespoons butter for brushing the waffle maker
- 6-8 eggs
- Salt and pepper
- 1 teaspoon Italian spice mix
- 1 tablespoon olive oil
- 1 tablespoon freshly chopped parsley

Directions:

1. Preheat the waffle maker.
2. Crack the eggs into a bowl and add the grated cheese.
3. Mix until just combined, then add the chopped spring onions and season with salt and pepper and dried garlic powder.
4. Stir in the almond flour and mix until everything is combined.
5. Brush the heated waffle maker with butter and add a few tablespoons of the batter.
6. Close the lid and cook for about 7–8 minutes depending on your waffle maker.
7. While the chaffles are cooking, prepare the scrambled eggs by whisking the eggs in a bowl until frothy, about 2 minutes. Season with salt and black pepper to taste and add the Italian spice mix. Whisk to blend in the spices.
8. Warm the oil in a non-stick pan over medium heat.
9. Pour the eggs in the pan and cook until eggs are set to your liking.
10. Serve each chaffle and top with some scrambled eggs. Top with freshly chopped parsley.

Nutrition Info: Per Serving Calories 194, fat 14.7 g, carbs 5 g, sugar 0.6 g, Protein 11.1 g, sodium 191 mg

Egg On A Cheddar Cheese Chaffle

Servings: 4
Cooking Time: 7–9 Minutes
Ingredients:

- Batter
- 4 eggs
- 2 cups shredded white cheddar cheese
- Salt and pepper to taste
- Other
- 2 tablespoons butter for brushing the waffle maker
- 4 large eggs
- 2 tablespoons olive oil

Directions:

1. Preheat the waffle maker.
2. Crack the eggs into a bowl and whisk them with a fork.
3. Stir in the grated cheddar cheese and season with salt and pepper.
4. Brush the heated waffle maker with butter and add a few tablespoons of the batter.
5. Close the lid and cook for about 7–8 minutes depending on your waffle maker.
6. While chaffles are cooking, cook the eggs.
7. Warm the oil in a large non-stick pan that has a lid over medium-low heat for 2-3 minutes
8. Crack an egg in a small ramekin and gently add it to the pan. Repeat the same way for the other 3 eggs.
9. Cover and let cook for 2 to 2 ½ minutes for set eggs but with runny yolks.
10. Remove from heat.
11. To serve, place a chaffle on each plate and top with an egg. Season with salt and black pepper to taste.

Nutrition Info: Per Serving Calories 412, fat 34 g, carbs 2 g, sugar 0.6 g, Protein 26 g, sodium 518 mg

Coconut Chaffles

Servings: 2
Cooking Time: 5 Minutes
Ingredients:

- 1 egg
- 1 oz. cream cheese,
- 1 oz. cheddar cheese
- 2 tbsps. coconut flour
- 1 tsp. stevia
- 1 tbsp. coconut oil, melted
- 1/2 tsp. coconut extract
- 2 eggs, soft boil for serving

Directions:

1. Heat you Dash waffle maker and grease with cooking spray.
2. Mix together all chaffles ingredients in a bowl.
3. Pour chaffle batter in a preheated waffle maker.
4. Close the lid.

5. Cook chaffles for about 2-3 minutes until golden brown.
6. Serve with boil egg and enjoy!

Nutrition Info: Per Serving: Protein: 21% 32 kcal Fat: 76% 117 kcal Carbohydrates: 3% 4 kcal

Garlic And Parsley Chaffles

Servings: 1
Cooking Time: 5 Minutes

Ingredients:

- 1 large egg
- 1/4 cup cheese mozzarella
- 1 tsp. coconut flour
- ¼ tsp. baking powder
- ½ tsp. garlic powder
- 1 tbsp. minutesced parsley
- For Serving
- 1 Poach egg
- 4 oz. smoked salmon

Directions:

1. Switch on your Dash waffle maker and let it preheat.
2. Grease waffle maker with cooking spray.
3. Mix together egg, mozzarella, coconut flour, baking powder, and garlic powder, parsley to a mixing bowl until combined well.
4. Pour batter in circle chaffle maker.
5. Close the lid.
6. Cook for about 2-3 minutes or until the chaffles are cooked.
7. Serve with smoked salmon and poached egg.
8. Enjoy!

Nutrition Info: Per Serving: Protein: 45% 140 kcal Fat: 51% 160 kcal Carbohydrates: 4% 14 kcal

LUNCH CHAFFLE RECIPES

Chaffle Egg Sandwich

Servings: 2
Cooking Time: 10 Minutes
Ingredients:

- 2 keto chaffle
- 2 slice cheddar cheese
- 1 egg simple omelet

Directions:

1. Prepare your oven on 400 F.
2. Arrange egg omelet and cheese slice between chaffles.
3. Bake in the preheated oven for about 4-5 minutes until cheese is melted.
4. Once the cheese is melted, remove from the oven.
5. Serve and enjoy!

Nutrition Info: Per Serving: Protein: 29% 144 kcal Fat: 68% 337 kcal Carbohydrates: 3% 14 kcal

Chaffles With Topping

Servings: 3
Cooking Time: 10 Minutes
Ingredients:

- 1 large egg
- 1 tbsp. almond flour
- 1 tbsp. full-fat Greek yogurt
- 1/8 tsp baking powder
- 1/4 cup shredded Swiss cheese
- TOPPING
- 4oz. grillprawns
- 4 oz. steamed cauliflower mash
- 1/2 zucchini sliced
- 3 lettuce leaves
- 1 tomato, sliced
- 1 tbsp. flax seeds

Directions:

1. Make 3 chaffles with the given chaffles ingredients.
2. For serving, arrange lettuce leaves on each chaffle.
3. Top with zucchini slice, grill prawns, cauliflower mash and a tomato slice.
4. Drizzle flax seeds on top.
5. Serve and enjoy!

Nutrition Info: Per Serving: Protein: 45% 71 kcal Fat: 47% 75 kcal Carbohydrates: 8% 12 kcal

Chaffle Cheese Sandwich

Servings: 1
Cooking Time: 10 Minutes

Ingredients:

- 2 square keto chaffle
- 2 slice cheddar cheese
- 2 lettuce leaves

Directions:

1. Prepare your oven on 400 F.
2. Arrange lettuce leave and cheese slice between chaffles.
3. Bake in the preheated oven for about 4-5 minutes until cheese is melted.
4. Once the cheese is melted, remove from the oven.
5. Serve and enjoy!

Nutrition Info: Per Serving: Protein: 28% 60 kcal Fat: 69% 149 kcal Carbohydrates: 3% 6 kcal

Chaffle Sandwich

Servings: 2
Cooking Time: 10 Minutes

Ingredients:

- 1 large egg
- 1/8 cup almond flour
- 1/2 tsp. garlic powder
- 3/4 tsp. baking powder
- 1/2 cup shredded cheese
- SANDWICH FILLING
- 2 slices deli ham
- 2 slices tomatoes
- 1 slice cheddar cheese

Directions:

1. Grease your square waffle maker and preheat it on medium heat.
2. Mix together chaffle ingredients in a mixing bowl until well combined.
3. Pour batter intoa square waffle and make two chaffles.
4. Once chaffles are cooked, remove from the maker.
5. For a sandwich,arrange deli ham, tomato slice and cheddar cheese between two chaffles.
6. Cut sandwich from the center.
7. Serve and enjoy!

Nutrition Info: Per Serving: Protein: 29% 70 kcal Fat: 66% 159 kcal Carbohydrates: 4% 10 kcal

Chicken Zinger Chaffle

Servings: 2
Cooking Time: 15 Minutes

Ingredients:

- 1 chicken breast, cut into 2 pieces
- 1/2 cup coconut flour
- 1/4 cup finely grated Parmesan
- 1 tsp. paprika
- 1/2 tsp. garlic powder
- 1/2 tsp. onion powder

- 1 tsp. salt& pepper
- 1 egg beaten
- Avocado oil for frying
- Lettuce leaves
- BBQ sauce
- CHAFFLE Ingredients:
- 4 oz. cheese
- 2 whole eggs
- 2 oz. almond flour
- 1/4 cup almond flour
- 1 tsp baking powder

Directions:

1. Mix together chaffle ingredients in a bowl.
2. Pour the chaffle batter in preheated greased square chaffle maker.
3. Cook chaffles for about 2-3 minutes until cooked through.
4. Make 4 square chaffles from this batter.
5. Meanwhile mix together coconut flour, parmesan, paprika, garlic powder, onion powder salt and pepper in a bowl.
6. Dip chicken first in coconut flour mixture then in beaten egg.
7. Heat avocado oil in a skillet and cook chicken from both sides. until lightly brown and cooked
8. Set chicken zinger between two chaffles with lettuce and BBQ sauce.
9. Enjoy!

Nutrition Info: Per Serving: Protein: 30% 219 kcal Fat: 60% 435 kcal Carbohydrates: 9% 66 kcal

Chaffle With Cheese & Bacon

Servings: 2
Cooking Time: 15 Minutes

Ingredients:

- 1 egg
- 1/2 cup cheddar cheese, shredded
- 1 tbsp. parmesan cheese
- 3/4 tsp coconut flour
- 1/4 tsp baking powder
- 1/8 tsp Italian Seasoning
- pinch of salt
- 1/4 tsp garlic powder
- FOR TOPPING
- 1 bacon sliced, cooked and chopped
- 1/2 cup mozzarella cheese, shredded
- 1/4 tsp parsley, chopped

Directions:

1. Preheat oven to 400 degrees.
2. Switch on your waffle maker and grease with cooking spray.
3. Mix together chaffle ingredients in a mixing bowl until combined.

4. Spoon half of the batter in the center of the waffle maker and close the lid. Cook chaffles for about 3-4 minutes until cooked.
5. Carefully remove chaffles from the maker.
6. Arrange chaffles in a greased baking tray.
7. Top with mozzarella cheese, chopped bacon and parsley.
8. And bake in the oven for 4 -5 minutes.
9. Once the cheese is melted, remove from the oven.
10. Serve and enjoy!

Nutrition Info: Per Serving: Protein: 28% 90 kcal Fat: 69% 222 kcal Carbohydrates: 3% 11 kcal

Chicken Bites With Chaffles

Servings: 2
Cooking Time:10 minutes

Ingredients:

- 1 chicken breastscut into 2 x2 inch chunks
- 1 egg, whisked
- 1/4 cup almond flour
- 2 tbsps. onion powder
- 2 tbsps. garlic powder
- 1 tsp. dried oregano
- 1 tsp. paprika powder
- 1 tsp. salt
- 1/2 tsp. black pepper
- 2 tbsps. avocado oil

Directions:

1. Add all the dry ingredients together into a large bowl.Mix well.
2. Place the eggs into a separate bowl.
3. Dip each chicken piece into the egg and then into the dry ingredients.
4. Heat oil in 10-inch skillet, add oil.
5. Once avocado oil is hot, place the coated chicken nuggets onto a skillet and cook for 6-8 minutes until cooked and golden brown.
6. Serve with chaffles and raspberries.
7. Enjoy!

Nutrition Info: Per Serving: Total Calories 401 kcal Fats 28.19 g Protein 32.35 g NetCarbs 1.46 g Fiber 3 g

Cauliflower Chaffles And Tomatoes

Servings: 2
Cooking Time: 15 Minutes

Ingredients:

- 1/2 cup cauliflower
- 1/4 tsp. garlic powder
- 1/4 tsp. black pepper
- 1/4 tsp. Salt
- 1/2 cup shredded cheddar cheese

- 1 egg
- FOR TOPPING
- 1 lettuce leave
- 1 tomato sliced
- 4 oz. cauliflower steamed, mashed
- 1 tsp sesame seeds

Directions:

1. Add all chaffle ingredients into a blender and mix well.
2. Sprinkle 1/8 shredded cheese on the waffle maker and pour cauliflower mixture in a preheated waffle maker and sprinkle the rest of the cheese over it.
3. Cook chaffles for about 4-5 minutes until cooked
4. For serving, lay lettuce leaves over chaffle top with steamed cauliflower and tomato.
5. Drizzle sesame seeds on top.
6. Enjoy!

Nutrition Info: Per Serving: Protein: 25% 49 kcal Fat: 65% 128 kcal Carbohydrates: 10% 21 kcal

Chaffle & Chicken Lunch Plate

Servings: 1
Cooking Time: 15 Minutes

Ingredients:

- 1 large egg
- 1/2 cup jack cheese, shredded
- 1 pinch salt
- For Serving
- 1 chicken leg
- salt
- pepper
- 1 tsp. garlic, minutesced
- 1 egg
- I tsp avocado oil

Directions:

1. Heat your square waffle maker and grease with cooking spray.
2. Pour Chaffle batter intothe skillet and cook for about 2-3 minutes.
3. Meanwhile,heat oil in a pan, over medium heat.
4. Once the oil is hot, add chicken thigh and garlicthen, cook for about 4-5 minutes. Flip and cook for another 3-4 minutes.
5. Season with salt and pepper and give them a good mix.
6. Transfer cooked thigh to plate.
7. Fry the egg in the same pan for about 1-2 minutes according to your choice.
8. Once chaffles are cooked, serve with fried egg and chicken thigh.
9. Enjoy!

Nutrition Info: Per Serving: Protein: 31% 138 kcal Fat: 66% 292 kcal Carbohydrates: 2% 10 kcal

Grill Pork Chaffle Sandwich

Servings: 2

Cooking Time: 15 Minutes

Ingredients:

- 1/2 cup mozzarella, shredded
- 1 egg
- I pinch garlic powder
- PORK PATTY
- 1/2 cup pork, minutesced
- 1 tbsp. green onion, diced
- 1/2 tsp Italian seasoning
- Lettuce leaves

Directions:

1. Preheat the square waffle maker and grease with
2. Mix together egg, cheese and garlic powder in a small mixing bowl.
3. Pour batter in a preheated waffle maker and close the lid.
4. Make 2 chaffles from thisbatter.
5. Cook chaffles for about 2-3 minutes until cooked through.
6. Meanwhile, mix together pork patty ingredients in a bowl and make 1 large patty.
7. Grill pork patty in a preheated grill for about 3-4 minutes per side until cooked through.
8. Arrange pork patty between two chaffles with lettuce leaves. Cut sandwich to make a triangular sandwich.
9. Enjoy!

Nutrition Info: Per Serving: Protein: 48% 85 kcal Fat: 48% 86 kcal Carbohydrates: 4% 7 kcal

Grill Beefsteak And Chaffle

Servings: 1

Cooking Time: 10 Minutes

Ingredients:

- 1 beefsteak rib eye
- 1 tsp salt
- 1 tsp pepper
- 1 tbsp. lime juice
- 1 tsp garlic

Directions:

1. Prepare your grill for direct heat.
2. Mix together all spices and rub over beefsteak evenly.
3. Place the beef on the grill rack over medium heat.
4. Cover and cook steak for about6 to 8 minutes. Flip and cook for another 4-5 minutes until cooked through.
5. Serve with keto simple chaffle and enjoy!

Nutrition Info: Per Serving: Protein: 51% 274 kcal Fat: 45% 243 kcal Carbohydrates: 4% 22 kcal

Crunchy Fish And Chaffle Bites

Servings: 4

Cooking Time: 15 Minutes

Ingredients:

- 1 lb. cod fillets, sliced into 4 slice
- 1 tsp. sea salt

- 1 tsp. garlic powder
- 1 egg, whisked
- 1 cup almond flour
- 2 tbsp. avocado oil
- CHAFFLE Ingredients:
- 2 eggs
- 1/2 cup cheddar cheese
- 2 tbsps. almond flour
- ½ tsp. Italian seasoning

Directions:

1. Mix together chaffle ingredients in a bowl and make 4 square
2. Put the chaffles in a preheated chaffle maker.
3. Mix together the salt, pepper, and garlic powder in a mixing bowl. Toss the cod cubes in this mixture and let sit for 10 minutes.
4. Then dip each cod slice into the egg mixture and then into the almond flour.
5. Heat oil in skillet and fish cubes for about 2-3 minutes, until cooked and browned
6. Serve on chaffles and enjoy!

Nutrition Info: Per Serving: Protein: 38% 121 kcal Fat: 59% 189 kcal Carbohydrates: 3% 11 kcal

Double Chicken Chaffles

Servings: 2
Cooking Time: 5 Minutes

Ingredients:

- 1/2 cup boil shredded chicken
- 1/4 cup cheddar cheese
- 1/8 cup parmesan cheese
- 1 egg
- 1 tsp. Italian seasoning
- 1/8 tsp. garlic powder
- 1 tsp. cream cheese

Directions:

1. Preheat the Belgian waffle maker.
2. Mix together in chaffle ingredients in a bowl and mix together.
3. Sprinkle 1 tbsp. of cheese in a waffle maker and pour in chaffle batter.
4. Pour 1 tbsp. of cheese over batter and close the lid.
5. Cook chaffles for about 4 to 5 minutes.
6. Serve with a chicken zinger and enjoy the double chicken flavor.

Nutrition Info: Per Serving: Protein: 30% 60 kcal Fat: 65% 129 kcal Carbohydrates: 5% 9 kcal

CHAFFLE MEAT RECIPES

Classic Beef Chaffle

Servings: 4
Cooking Time: 10 Minutes
Ingredients:

- Batter
- ½ pound ground beef
- 4 eggs
- 4 ounces cream cheese
- 1 cup grated mozzarella cheese
- Salt and pepper to taste
- 1 clove garlic, minced
- ½ teaspoon freshly chopped rosemary
- Other
- 2 tablespoons butter to brush the waffle maker
- ¼ cup sour cream
- 2 tablespoons freshly chopped parsley for garnish

Directions:

1. Preheat the waffle maker.
2. Add the ground beef, eggs, cream cheese, grated mozzarella cheese, salt and pepper, minced garlic and freshly chopped rosemary to a bowl.
3. Brush the heated waffle maker with butter and add a few tablespoons of the batter.
4. Close the lid and cook for about 8–10 minutes depending on your waffle maker.
5. Serve each chaffle with a tablespoon of sour cream and freshly chopped parsley on top.
6. Serve and enjoy.

Nutrition Info: Per Serving Calories 368, fat 27.4 g, carbs 2.1 g, sugar 0.4 g, Protein 27.4 g, sodium 291 mg

Beef Chaffle Tower

Servings: 4
Cooking Time: 15 Minutes
Ingredients:

- Batter
- 4 eggs
- 2 cups grated mozzarella cheese
- Salt and pepper to taste
- 2 tablespoons almond flour
- 1 teaspoon Italian seasoning
- Beef
- 2 tablespoons butter
- 1 pound beef tenderloin
- Salt and pepper to taste
- 1 teaspoon chili flakes
- Other
- 2 tablespoons cooking spray to brush the waffle maker

Directions:

1. Preheat the waffle maker.
2. Add the eggs, grated mozzarella cheese, salt and pepper, almond flour and Italian seasoning to a bowl.
3. Mix until everything is fully combined.
4. Brush the heated waffle maker with cooking spray and add a few tablespoons of the batter.
5. Close the lid and cook for about 5–7 minutes depending on your waffle maker.
6. Meanwhile, heat the butter in a nonstick frying pan and season the beef tenderloin with salt and pepper and chili flakes.
7. Cook the beef tenderloin for about 5–7 minutes on each side.
8. When serving, assemble the chaffle tower by placing one chaffle on a plate, a layer of diced beef tenderloin, another chaffle, another layer of beef, and so on until you finish with the chaffles and beef.
9. Serve and enjoy.

Nutrition Info: Per Serving Calories 412, fat 25 g, carbs 1.8 g, sugar 0.5 g, Protein 43.2 g, sodium 256 mg

Turkey Bbq Sauce Chaffle

Servings: 4
Cooking Time: 8–10 Minutes

Ingredients:

- Batter
- ½ pound ground turkey meat
- 3 eggs
- 1 cup grated Swiss cheese
- ¼ cup cream cheese
- ¼ cup BBQ sauce
- 1 teaspoon dried oregano
- Salt and pepper to taste
- 2 cloves garlic, minced
- Other
- 2 tablespoons butter to brush the waffle maker
- ¼ cup BBQ sauce for serving
- 2 tablespoons freshly chopped parsley for garnish

Directions:

1. Preheat the waffle maker.
2. Add the ground turkey, eggs, grated Swiss cheese, cream cheese, BBQ sauce, dried oregano, salt and pepper, and minced garlic to a bowl.
3. Mix everything until combined and batter forms.
4. Brush the heated waffle maker with butter and add a few tablespoons of the batter.
5. Close the lid and cook for about 8–10 minutes depending on your waffle maker.
6. Serve each chaffle with a tablespoon of BBQ sauce and a sprinkle of freshly chopped parsley.

Nutrition Info: Per Serving Calories 365, fat 23.7 g, carbs 13.7 g, sugar 8.8 g, Protein 23.5 g, sodium 595 mg

Beef And Tomato Chaffle

Servings: 4
Cooking Time: 15 Minutes
Ingredients:

- Batter
- 4 eggs
- ¼ cup cream cheese
- 1 cup grated mozzarella cheese
- Salt and pepper to taste
- ¼ cup almond flour
- 1 teaspoon freshly chopped dill
- Beef
- 1 pound beef loin
- Salt and pepper to taste
- 1 tablespoon balsamic vinegar
- 2 tablespoons olive oil
- 1 teaspoon freshly chopped rosemary
- Other
- 2 tablespoons cooking spray to brush the waffle maker
- 4 tomato slices for serving

Directions:

1. Preheat the waffle maker.
2. Add the eggs, cream cheese, grated mozzarella cheese, salt and pepper, almond flour and freshly chopped dill to a bowl.
3. Mix until combined and batter forms.
4. Brush the heated waffle maker with cooking spray and add a few tablespoons of the batter.
5. Close the lid and cook for about 8–10 minutes depending on your waffle maker.
6. Meanwhile, heat the olive oil in a nonstick frying pan and season the beef loin with salt and pepper and freshly chopped rosemary.
7. Cook the beef on each side for about 5 minutes and drizzle with some balsamic vinegar.
8. Serve each chaffle with a slice of tomato and cooked beef loin slices.

Nutrition Info: Per Serving Calories 492, fat 35.8 g, carbs 3.3 g, sugar 0.8 g, Protein 40.3 g, sodium 200 mg

Chicken Taco Chaffle

Servings: 4
Cooking Time: 15 Minutes
Ingredients:

- Batter
- 4 eggs
- 2 cups grated provolone cheese
- 6 tablespoons almond flour
- 2½ teaspoons baking powder
- Salt and pepper to taste
- Chicken topping
- 2 tablespoons olive oil

- ½ pound ground chicken
- Salt and pepper to taste
- 1 garlic clove, minced
- 2 teaspoons dried oregano
- Other
- 2 tablespoons butter to brush the waffle maker
- 2 tablespoons freshly chopped spring onion for garnishing

Directions:

1. Preheat the waffle maker.
2. Add the eggs, grated provolone cheese, almond flour, baking powder and salt and pepper to a bowl.
3. Mix until just combined.
4. Brush the heated waffle maker with cooking spray and add a few tablespoons of the batter.
5. Close the lid and cook for about 7–9 minutes depending on your waffle maker.
6. Meanwhile, heat the olive oil in a nonstick pan over medium heat and start cooking the ground chicken.
7. Season with salt and pepper and stir in the minced garlic and dried oregano. Cook for 10 minutes.
8. Add some of the cooked ground chicken to each chaffle and serve with freshly chopped spring onion.

Nutrition Info: Per Serving Calories 584, fat 44 g, carbs 6.4 g, sugar 0.8 g, Protein 41.3g, sodium 737 mg

Garlic Chicken Chaffle

Servings: 4
Cooking Time: 15 Minutes

Ingredients:

- Batter
- 4 eggs
- 2 cups grated mozzarella cheese
- ¼ cup almond flour
- 2 tablespoons coconut flour
- 2½ teaspoons baking powder
- Salt and pepper to taste
- Garlic Chicken Topping
- 1 pound diced chicken
- Salt and pepper to taste
- 1 teaspoon dried oregano
- 2 garlic cloves, minced
- 3 tablespoons butter
- Other
- 2 tablespoons cooking spray for greasing the waffle maker
- 2 tablespoons freshly chopped parsley

Directions:

1. Preheat the waffle maker.

2. Add the eggs, grated mozzarella cheese, almond flour, coconut flour and baking powder to a bowl and season with salt and pepper.
3. Mix until just combined.
4. Spray the waffle maker with cooking spray to prevent the chaffles from sticking. Add a few tablespoons of the batter to the heated and greased waffle maker.
5. Close the lid and cook for about 5–7 minutes depending on your waffle maker.
6. Repeat with the rest of the batter.
7. Meanwhile, melt the butter in a nonstick pan over medium heat.
8. Season the chicken with salt and pepper and dried oregano and mix in the minced garlic.
9. Cook the chicken for about 10 minutes, stirring constantly.
10. Serve each chaffle with a topping of the garlic chicken mixture and sprinkle some freshly chopped parsley on top.

Nutrition Info: Per Serving Calories 475, fat 29.5 g, carbs 7.2 g, sugar 0.4 g, Protein 44.7 g, sodium 286 mg

Rosemary Pork Chops On Chaffle

Servings: 4
Cooking Time: 15 Minutes

Ingredients:

- 4 eggs
- 2 cups grated mozzarella cheese
- Salt and pepper to taste
- Pinch of nutmeg
- 2 tablespoons sour cream
- 6 tablespoons almond flour
- 2 teaspoons baking powder
- Pork chops
- 2 tablespoons olive oil
- 1 pound pork chops
- Salt and pepper to taste
- 1 teaspoon freshly chopped rosemary
- Other
- 2 tablespoons cooking spray to brush the waffle maker
- 2 tablespoons freshly chopped basil for decoration

Directions:

1. Preheat the waffle maker.
2. Add the eggs, mozzarella cheese, salt and pepper, nutmeg, sour cream, almond flour and baking powder to a bowl.
3. Mix until combined.
4. Brush the heated waffle maker with cooking spray and add a few tablespoons of the batter.
5. Close the lid and cook for about 5–7 minutes depending on your waffle maker.
6. Meanwhile, heat the butter in a nonstick grill pan and season the pork chops with salt and pepper and freshly chopped rosemary.
7. Cook the pork chops for about 4–5 minutes on each side.
8. Serve each chaffle with a pork chop and sprinkle some freshly chopped basil on top.

Nutrition Info: Per Serving Calories 666, fat 55.2 g, carbs 4.8 g, sugar 0.4 g, Protein 37.5 g, sodium 235 mg

Beef And Sour Cream Chaffle

Servings: 4
Cooking Time: 15 Minutes
Ingredients:

- Batter
- 4 eggs
- 2 cups grated mozzarella cheese
- 3 tablespoons coconut flour
- 3 tablespoons almond flour
- 2 teaspoons baking powder
- Salt and pepper to taste
- 1 tablespoon freshly chopped parsley
- Seasoned beef
- 1 pound beef tenderloin
- Salt and pepper to taste
- 2 tablespoons olive oil
- 1 tablespoon Dijon mustard
- Other
- 2 tablespoons olive oil to brush the waffle maker
- ¼ cup sour cream for garnish
- 2 tablespoons freshly chopped spring onion for garnish

Directions:

1. Preheat the waffle maker.
2. Add the eggs, grated mozzarella cheese, coconut flour, almond flour, baking powder, salt and pepper and freshly chopped parsley to a bowl.
3. Mix until just combined and batter forms.
4. Brush the heated waffle maker with olive oil and add a few tablespoons of the batter.
5. Close the lid and cook for about 5–7 minutes depending on your waffle maker.
6. Meanwhile, heat the olive oil in a nonstick pan over medium heat.
7. Season the beef tenderloin with salt and pepper and spread the whole piece of beef tenderloin with Dijon mustard.
8. Cook on each side for about 4–5 minutes.
9. Serve each chaffle with sour cream and slices of the cooked beef tenderloin.
10. Garnish with freshly chopped spring onion.
11. Serve and enjoy.

Nutrition Info: Per Serving Calories 543, fat 37 g, carbs 7.9 g, sugar 0.5 g, Protein 44.9 g, sodium 269 mg

Classic Ground Pork Chaffle

Servings: 4
Cooking Time: 15 Minutes
Ingredients:

- ½ pound ground pork
- 3 eggs

- ½ cup grated mozzarella cheese
- Salt and pepper to taste
- 1 clove garlic, minced
- 1 teaspoon dried oregano
- Other
- 2 tablespoons butter to brush the waffle maker
- 2 tablespoons freshly chopped parsley for garnish

Directions:

1. Preheat the waffle maker.
2. Add the ground pork, eggs, mozzarella cheese, salt and pepper, minced garlic and dried oregano to a bowl.
3. Mix until combined.
4. Brush the heated waffle maker with butter and add a few tablespoons of the batter.
5. Close the lid and cook for about 7–8 minutes depending on your waffle maker.
6. Serve with freshly chopped parsley.

Nutrition Info: Per Serving Calories 192, fat 11.7 g, carbs 1 g, sugar 0.3 g, Protein 20.2 g, sodium 142 mg

Pork Tzatziki Chaffle

Servings: 4
Cooking Time: 25 Minutes

Ingredients:

- 4 eggs
- 2 cups grated provolone cheese
- Salt and pepper to taste
- 1 teaspoon dried rosemary
- 1 teaspoon dried oregano
- Pork loin
- 2 tablespoons olive oil
- 1 pound pork tenderloin
- Salt and pepper to taste
- Tzatziki sauce
- 1 cup sour cream
- Salt and pepper to taste
- 1 cucumber, peeled and diced
- 1 teaspoon garlic powder
- 1 teaspoon dried dill
- Other
- 2 tablespoons butter to brush the waffle maker

Directions:

1. Preheat the waffle maker.
2. Add the eggs, grated provolone cheese, dried rosemary, and dried oregano to a bowl. Season with salt and pepper to taste.
3. Mix until combined.
4. Brush the heated waffle maker with butter and add a few tablespoons of the batter.
5. Close the lid and cook for about 5—7 minutes depending on your waffle maker.

6. Meanwhile, heat the olive oil in a nonstick frying pan. Generously season the pork tenderloin with salt and pepper and cook it for about 7 minutes on each side.
7. Mix the sour cream, salt and pepper, diced cucumber, garlic powder and dried dill in a bowl.
8. Serve each chaffle with a few tablespoons of tzatziki sauce and slices of pork tenderloin.

Nutrition Info: Per Serving Calories 700, fat 50.9 g, carbs 6 g, sugar 1.5 g, Protein 54.4 g, sodium 777 mg

Beef Meatza Chaffle

Servings: 4
Cooking Time: 15 Minutes
Ingredients:

- Meatza chaffle batter
- ½ pound ground beef
- 4 eggs
- 2 cups grated cheddar cheese
- Salt and pepper to taste
- 1 teaspoon Italian seasoning
- 2 tablespoons tomato sauce
- Other
- 2 tablespoons cooking spray to brush the waffle maker
- ¼ cup tomato sauce for serving
- 2 tablespoons freshly chopped basil for serving

Directions:

1. Preheat the waffle maker.
2. Add the ground beef, eggs, grated cheddar cheese, salt and pepper, Italian seasoning and tomato sauce to a bowl.
3. Mix until everything is fully combined.
4. Brush the heated waffle maker with cooking spray and add a few tablespoons of the batter.
5. Close the lid and cook for about 7–10 minutes depending on your waffle maker.
6. Serve with tomato sauce and freshly chopped basil on top.

Nutrition Info: Per Serving Calories 470, fat 34.6 g, carbs 2.5 g, sugar 1.7 g, Protein 36.5 g, sodium 581 mg

Bbq Sauce Pork Chaffle

Servings: 4
Cooking Time: 15 Minutes
Ingredients:

- ½ pound ground pork
- 3 eggs
- 1 cup grated mozzarella cheese
- Salt and pepper to taste
- 1 clove garlic, minced
- 1 teaspoon dried rosemary
- 3 tablespoons sugar-free BBQ sauce
- Other

- 2 tablespoons butter to brush the waffle maker
- ½ pound pork rinds for serving
- ¼ cup sugar-free BBQ sauce for serving

Directions:

1. Preheat the waffle maker.
2. Add the ground pork, eggs, mozzarella, salt and pepper, minced garlic, dried rosemary, and BBQ sauce to a bowl.
3. Mix until combined.
4. Brush the heated waffle maker with butter and add a few tablespoons of the batter.
5. Close the lid and cook for about 7–8 minutes depending on your waffle maker.
6. Serve each chaffle with some pork rinds and a tablespoon of BBQ sauce.

Nutrition Info: Per Serving Calories 350, fat 21.1 g, carbs 2.7 g, sugar 0.3 g, Protein 36.9 g, sodium 801 mg

Beef Chaffle Sandwich Recipe

Servings: 4
Cooking Time: 15 Minutes

Ingredients:

- Batter
- 3 eggs
- 2 cups grated mozzarella cheese
- ¼ cup cream cheese
- Salt and pepper to taste
- 1 teaspoon Italian seasoning
- Beef
- 2 tablespoons butter
- 1 pound beef tenderloin
- Salt and pepper to taste
- 2 teaspoons Dijon mustard
- 1 teaspoon dried paprika
- Other
- 2 tablespoons cooking spray to brush the waffle maker
- 4 lettuce leaves for serving
- 4 tomato slices for serving
- 4 leaves fresh basil

Directions:

1. Preheat the waffle maker.
2. Add the eggs, grated mozzarella cheese, salt and pepper and Italian seasoning to a bowl.
3. Mix until combined and batter forms.
4. Brush the heated waffle maker with cooking spray and add a few tablespoons of the batter.
5. Close the lid and cook for about 5–7 minutes depending on your waffle maker.
6. Meanwhile, melt and heat the butter in a nonstick frying pan.
7. Season the beef loin with salt and pepper, brush it with Dijon mustard, and sprinkle some dried paprika on top.
8. Cook the beef on each side for about 5 minutes.
9. Thinly slice the beef and assemble the chaffle sandwiches.

10. Cut each chaffle in half and on one half place a lettuce leaf, tomato slice, basil leaf, and some sliced beef.
11. Cover with the other chaffle half and serve.
Nutrition Info: Per Serving Calories 477, fat 32.8g, carbs 2.3 g, sugar 0.9 g, Protein 42.2 g, sodium 299 mg

Ground Chicken Chaffle

Servings: 4
Cooking Time: 8–10 Minutes
Ingredients:
- Batter
- ½ pound ground chicken
- 4 eggs
- 3 tablespoons tomato sauce
- Salt and pepper to taste
- 1 cup grated mozzarella cheese
- 1 teaspoon dried oregano
- Other
- 2 tablespoons butter to brush the waffle maker

Directions:
1. Preheat the waffle maker.
2. Add the ground chicken, eggs and tomato sauce to a bowl and season with salt and pepper.
3. Mix everything with a fork and stir in the mozzarella cheese and dried oregano.
4. Mix again until fully combined.
5. Brush the heated waffle maker with butter and add a few tablespoons of the batter.
6. Close the lid and cook for about 8–10 minutes depending on your waffle maker.
7. Serve and enjoy.

Nutrition Info: Per Serving Calories 246, fat 15.6 g, carbs 1.5 g, sugar 0.9 g, Protein 24.2 g, sodium 254 mg

Italian Chicken And Basil Chaffle

Servings: 4
Cooking Time: 7–9 Minutes
Ingredients:
- Batter
- ½ pound ground chicken
- 4 eggs
- 3 tablespoons tomato sauce
- Salt and pepper to taste
- 1 cup grated mozzarella cheese
- 1 teaspoon dried oregano
- 3 tablespoons freshly chopped basil leaves
- ½ teaspoon dried garlic
- Other
- 2 tablespoons butter to brush the waffle maker

- ¼ cup tomato sauce for serving
- 1 tablespoon freshly chopped basil for serving

Directions:

1. Preheat the waffle maker.
2. Add the ground chicken, eggs and tomato sauce to a bowl and season with salt and pepper.
3. Add the mozzarella cheese and season with dried oregano, freshly chopped basil and dried garlic.
4. Mix until fully combined and batter forms.
5. Brush the heated waffle maker with butter and add a few tablespoons of the chaffle batter.
6. Close the lid and cook for about 7–9 minutes depending on your waffle maker.
7. Repeat with the rest of the batter.
8. Serve with tomato sauce and freshly chopped basil on top.

Nutrition Info: Per Serving Calories 250, fat 15.7 g, carbs 2.5 g, sugar 1.5 g, Protein 24.5 g, sodium 334 mg

Pork Loin Chaffle Sandwich

Servings: 4
Cooking Time: 15 Minutes

Ingredients:

- 4 eggs
- 1 cup grated mozzarella cheese
- 1 cup grated parmesan cheese
- Salt and pepper to taste
- 2 tablespoons cream cheese
- 6 tablespoons coconut flour
- 2 teaspoons baking powder
- Pork loin
- 2 tablespoons olive oil
- 1 pound pork loin
- Salt and pepper to taste
- 2 cloves garlic, minced
- 1 tablespoon freshly chopped thyme
- Other
- 2 tablespoons cooking spray to brush the waffle maker
- 4 lettuce leaves for serving
- 4 slices of tomato for serving
- ¼ cup sugar-free mayonnaise for serving

Directions:

1. Preheat the waffle maker.
2. Add the eggs, mozzarella cheese, parmesan cheese, salt and pepper, cream cheese, coconut flour and baking powder to a bowl.
3. Mix until combined.
4. Brush the heated waffle maker with cooking spray and add a few tablespoons of the batter.
5. Close the lid and cook for about 5–7 minutes depending on your waffle maker.
6. Meanwhile, heat the olive oil in a nonstick frying pan and season the pork loin with salt and pepper, minced garlic and freshly chopped thyme.

7. Cook the pork loin for about 5–7 minutes on each side.
8. Cut each chaffle in half and add some mayonnaise, lettuce leaf, tomato slice and sliced pork loin on one half.
9. Cover the sandwich with the other chaffle half and serve.

Nutrition Info: Per Serving Calories 710, fat 52.7 g, carbs 11.3 g, sugar 0.8 g, Protein 47.4 g, sodium 513 mg

Creamy Bacon Salad On A Chaffle

Servings: 4
Cooking Time: 15 Minutes

Ingredients:

- 4 eggs
- 1½ cups grated mozzarella cheese
- ½ cup parmesan cheese
- Salt and pepper to taste
- 1 teaspoon dried oregano
- ¼ cup almond flour
- 2 teaspoons baking powder
- Bacon salad
- ½ pound cooked bacon
- 1 cup cream cheese
- 1 teaspoon dried oregano
- 1 teaspoon dried basil
- 1 teaspoon dried rosemary
- 2 tablespoons lemon juice
- Other
- 2 tablespoons butter to brush the waffle maker
- 2 spring onions, finely chopped, for serving

Directions:

1. Preheat the waffle maker.
2. Add the eggs, mozzarella cheese, parmesan cheese, salt and pepper, dried oregano, almond flour and baking powder to a bowl.
3. Mix until combined.
4. Brush the heated waffle maker with butter and add a few tablespoons of the batter.
5. Close the lid and cook for about 5–7 minutes depending on your waffle maker.
6. Meanwhile, chop the cooked bacon into smaller pieces and place them in a bowl with the cream cheese. Season with dried oregano, dried basil, dried rosemary and lemon juice.
7. Mix until combined and spread each chaffle with the creamy bacon salad.
8. To serve, sprinkle some freshly chopped spring onion on top.

Nutrition Info: Per Serving Calories 750, fat 62.5 g, carbs 7.7 g, sugar 0.8 g, Protein 40.3 g, sodium 1785 mg

SIMPLE CHAFFLE RECIPES

Cream Cheese Chaffle

Servings: 2
Cooking Time: 8 Minutes

Ingredients:

- 1 egg, beaten
- 1 oz. cream cheese
- ½ teaspoon vanilla
- 4 teaspoons sweetener
- ¼ teaspoon baking powder
- Cream cheese

Directions:

1. Preheat your waffle maker.
2. Add all the ingredients in a bowl.
3. Mix well.
4. Pour half of the batter into the waffle maker.
5. Seal the device.
6. Cook for 4 minutes.
7. Remove the chaffle from the waffle maker.
8. Make the second one using the same steps.
9. Spread remaining cream cheese on top before serving.

Nutrition Info: Calories 169Total Fat 14.3g Saturated Fat 7.6g Cholesterol 195mg Sodium 147mg Potassium 222mgTotal Carbohydrate 4g Dietary Fiber 4g Protein 7.7g Total Sugars 0.7g

Chaffles With Almond Flour

Servings: 4
Cooking Time: 5 Minutes

Ingredients:

- 2 large eggs
- 1/4 cup almond flour
- 3/4 tsp baking powder
- 1 cup cheddar cheese, shredded
- Cooking spray

Directions:

1. Switch on your waffle maker and grease with cooking spray.
2. Beat eggs with almond flour and baking powder in a mixing bowl.
3. Once the eggs and cheese are mixed together, add in cheese and mix again.
4. Pour 1/4 cup of the batter in the dash mini waffle maker and close the lid.
5. Cook chaffles for about 2-3 minutes until crispy and cooked
6. Repeat with the remaining batter
7. Carefully transfer the chafflesto plate.
8. Serve with almonds and enjoy!

Nutrition Info: Per Serving: Protein: 23% 52 kcal Fat: 72% 159 kcal Carbohydrates: 5% 11 kcal

Chaffle With Sausage Gravy

Servings: 2
Cooking Time: 15 Minutes
Ingredients:

- ¼ cup sausage, cooked
- 3 tablespoons chicken broth
- 2 teaspoons cream cheese
- 2 tablespoons heavy whipping cream
- ¼ teaspoon garlic powder
- Pepper to taste
- 2 basic chaffles

Directions:

1. Add the sausage, broth, cream cheese, cream, garlic powder and pepper to a pan over medium heat.
2. Bring to a boil and then reduce heat.
3. Simmer for 10 minutes or until the sauce has thickened.
4. Pour the gravy on top of the basic chaffles
5. Serve.

Nutrition Info: Calories 212Total Fat 17 g Saturated Fat 10 g Cholesterol 134 mg Sodium 350 mg Potassium 133 mgTotal Carbohydrate 3 g Dietary Fiber 1 g Protein 11 g Total Sugars 1 g

Mozzarella & Almond Flour Chaffles

Servings: 2
Cooking Time: 8 Minutes
Ingredients:

- ½ cup Mozzarella cheese, shredded
- 1 large organic egg
- 2 tablespoons blanched almond flour
- ¼ teaspoon organic baking powder

Directions:

1. Preheat a mini waffle iron and then grease it.
2. In a medium bowl, place all ingredients and with a fork, mix until well combined.
3. Place half of the mixture into preheated waffle iron and cook for about 3-4 minutes or until golden brown.
4. Repeat with the remaining mixture.
5. Serve warm.

Nutrition Info: Per Serving Calories: 98 Net Carb: 1.4g Fat: 7.1g Saturated Fat: 1g Carbohydrates: 2.2g Dietary Fiber: 0.8g Sugar: 0.2g Protein: 6.7g

Pumpkin & Pecan Chaffle

Servings: 2
Cooking Time: 10 Minutes
Ingredients:

- 1 egg, beaten
- ½ cup mozzarella cheese, grated

- ½ teaspoon pumpkin spice
- 1 tablespoon pureed pumpkin
- 2 tablespoons almond flour
- 1 teaspoon sweetener
- 2 tablespoons pecans, chopped

Directions:

1. Turn on the waffle maker.
2. Beat the egg in a bowl.
3. Stir in the rest of the ingredients.
4. Pour half of the mixture into the device.
5. Seal the lid.
6. Cook for 5 minutes.
7. Remove the chaffle carefully.
8. Repeat the steps to make the second chaffle.

Nutrition Info: Calories 210Total Fat 17 g Saturated Fat 10 g Cholesterol 110 mg Sodium 250 mg Potassium 570 mgTotal Carbohydrate 4.6 g Dietary Fiber 1.7 g Protein 11 g Total Sugars 2 g

Double Choco Chaffle

Servings: 2
Cooking Time: 10 Minutes

Ingredients:

- 1 egg
- 2 teaspoons coconut flour
- 2 tablespoons sweetener
- 1 tablespoon cocoa powder
- ¼ teaspoon baking powder
- 1 oz. cream cheese
- ½ teaspoon vanilla
- 1 tablespoon sugar-free chocolate chips

Directions:

1. Put all the ingredients in a large bowl.
2. Mix well.
3. Pour half of the mixture into the waffle maker.
4. Seal the device.
5. Cook for 4 minutes.
6. Uncover and transfer to a plate to cool.
7. Repeat the procedure to make the second chaffle.

Nutrition Info: Calories 171Total Fat 10.7g Saturated Fat 5.3g Cholesterol 97mg Sodium 106mg Potassium 179mgTotal Carbohydrate 3g Dietary Fiber 4.8g Protein 5.8g Total Sugars 0.4g

Brie And Blackberry Chaffles

Servings: 4
Cooking Time: 36 Minutes

Ingredients:

- For the chaffles:
- 2 eggs, beaten
- 1 cup finely grated mozzarella cheese
- For the topping:
- 1 ½ cups blackberries
- 1 lemon, 1 tsp zest and 2 tbsp juice
- 1 tbsp erythritol
- 4 slices Brie cheese

Directions:

1. For the chaffles:
2. Preheat the waffle iron.
3. Meanwhile, in a medium bowl, mix the eggs and mozzarella cheese.
4. Open the iron, pour in a quarter of the mixture, cover, and cook until crispy, 7 minutes.
5. Remove the chaffle onto a plate and make 3 more with the remaining batter.
6. Plate and set aside.
7. For the topping:
8. In a medium pot, add the blackberries, lemon zest, lemon juice, and erythritol. Cook until the blackberries break and the sauce thickens, 5 minutes. Turn the heat off.
9. Arrange the chaffles on the baking sheet and place two Brie cheese slices on each. Top with blackberry mixture and transfer the baking sheet to the oven.
10. Bake until the cheese melts, 2 to 3 minutes.
11. Remove from the oven, allow cooling and serve afterward.

Nutrition Info: Calories 576Fats 42.22gCarbs 7.07gNet Carbs 3.67g Protein 42.35g

Cinnamon Powder Chaffles

Servings: 2
Cooking Time: 5 Minutes

Ingredients:

- 1 large egg
- 3/4 cup cheddar cheese, shredded
- 2 tbsps. coconut flour
- 1/2 tbsps. coconut oil melted
- 1 tsp. stevia
- 1/2 tsp cinnamon powder
- 1/2 tsp vanilla extract
- 1/2 tsp psyllium husk powder
- 1/4 tsp baking powder

Directions:

1. Switch on your waffle maker.
2. Grease your waffle maker with cooking spray and heat up on medium heat.
3. In a mixing bowl, beat egg withcoconut flour, oil, stevia, cinnamon powder, vanilla, husk powder, and baking powder.
4. Once the egg is beaten well, add in cheeseand mix again.
5. Pour half of the waffle batter into the middle of your waffle iron and close the lid.
6. Cook chaffles for about 2-3 minutes until crispy.
7. Once chaffles are cooked, carefully remove them from the maker.

8. Serve with keto hot chocolate and enjoy!

Nutrition Info: Per Serving: Protein: 25% 62 kcal Fat: 72% 175 kcal Carbohydrates: 3% 7 kcal

Savory Beef Chaffle

Servings: 2
Cooking Time: 15 Minutes

Ingredients:

- 1 teaspoon olive oil
- 2 cups ground beef
- Garlic salt to taste
- 1 red bell pepper, sliced into strips
- 1 green bell pepper, sliced into strips
- 1 onion, minced
- 1 bay leaf
- 2 garlic chaffles
- Butter

Directions:

1. Put your pan over medium heat.
2. Add the olive oil and cook ground beef until brown.
3. Season with garlic salt and add bay leaf.
4. Drain the fat, transfer to a plate and set aside.
5. Discard the bay leaf.
6. In the same pan, cook the onion and bell peppers for 2 minutes.
7. Put the beef back to the pan.
8. Heat for 1 minute.
9. Spread butter on top of the chaffle.
10. Add the ground beef and veggies.
11. Roll or fold the chaffle.

Nutrition Info: Calories 220Total Fat 17.8g Saturated Fat 8g Cholesterol 76mg Sodium 60mg Total Carbohydrate 3g Dietary Fiber 2g Total Sugars 5.4g Protein 27.1g Potassium 537mg

Pumpkin Chaffles

Servings: 2
Cooking Time: 5 Minutes

Ingredients:

- 1/2 oz. cream cheese
- 1 large egg
- 1/2 cup cheddar cheese, shredded
- 2 tbsps. pumpkin puree
- 1 tsp. stevia
- 3 tsps. coconut flour
- 1/2 tbsps. pumpkin pie spice
- 1/2 tsp vanilla extract
- 1/4 tsp baking powder

Directions:

1. Grease your Belgian waffle maker with cooking spray and switch it on.
2. Crack the egg in a mixing bowl containingcoconut flour, pumpkin spice, stevia, pumpkin spice, vanilla extract, and baking powder. Mix thoroughly.
3. Once the ingredients are mixed together with egg, add in cheese and mix again.
4. Pour half of the chaffles batter into the middle of your waffle iron and close the lid.
5. Cook chaffles for about 2-3 minutes until cooked and light golden.
6. Repeat with the remaining batter
7. Once chaffles are cooked, remove from the maker.
8. Serve with BLT coffee and enjoy!

Nutrition Info: Per Serving: Protein: 19% 50 kcal Fat: 72% 185 kcal Carbohydrates: 9% 23 kcal

Okonomiyaki Chaffles

Servings: 4
Cooking Time: 28 Minutes

Ingredients:

- For the chaffles:
- 2 eggs, beaten
- 1 cup finely grated mozzarella cheese
- ½ tsp baking powder
- ¼ cup shredded radishes
- For the sauce:
- 2 tsp coconut aminos
- 2 tbsp sugar-free ketchup
- 1 tbsp sugar-free maple syrup
- 2 tsp Worcestershire sauce
- For the topping:
- 1 tbsp mayonnaise
- 2 tbsp chopped fresh scallions
- 2 tbsp bonito flakes
- 1 tsp dried seaweed powder
- 1 tbsp pickled ginger

Directions:

1. For the chaffles:
2. Preheat the waffle iron.
3. In a medium bowl, mix the eggs, mozzarella cheese, baking powder, and radishes.
4. Open the iron and add a quarter of the mixture. Close and cook until crispy, 7 minutes.
5. Transfer the chaffle to a plate and make a 3 more chaffles in the same manner.
6. For the sauce:
7. Combine the coconut aminos, ketchup, maple syrup, and Worcestershire sauce in a medium bowl and mix well.
8. For the topping:
9. In another mixing bowl, mix the mayonnaise, scallions, bonito flakes, seaweed powder, and ginger
10. To Servings:

11. Arrange the chaffles on four different plates and swirl the sauce on top. Spread the topping on the chaffles and serve afterward.
Nutrition Info: Calories 90Fats 3.32gCarbs 2.97gNet Carbs 2.17g Protein 12.09g

Mozzarellas & Psyllium Husk Chaffles

Servings: 2
Cooking Time: 8 Minutes
Ingredients:
- ½ cup Mozzarella cheese, shredded
- 1 large organic egg, beaten
- 2 tablespoons blanched almond flour
- ½ teaspoon Psyllium husk powder
- ¼ teaspoon organic baking powder

Directions:
1. Preheat a mini waffle iron and then grease it.
2. In a bowl, place all the ingredients and beat until well combined.
3. Place half of the mixture into preheated waffle iron and cook for about 3-4 minutes or until golden brown.
4. Repeat with the remaining mixture.
5. Serve warm.

Nutrition Info: Per Serving Calories: 101Net Carb: 1.6gFat: 7.1gSaturated Fat: 1.8g Carbohydrates: 2.9gDietary Fiber: 1.3g Sugar: 0.2g Protein: 6.7g

Carrot Chaffle Cake

Servings: 6
Cooking Time: 24 Minutes
Ingredients:
- 1 egg, beaten
- 2 tablespoons melted butter
- ½ cup carrot, shredded
- ¾ cup almond flour
- 1 teaspoon baking powder
- 2 tablespoons heavy whipping cream
- 2 tablespoons sweetener
- 1 tablespoon walnuts, chopped
- 1 teaspoon pumpkin spice
- 2 teaspoons cinnamon

Directions:
1. Preheat your waffle maker.
2. In a large bowl, combine all the ingredients.
3. Pour some of the mixture into the waffle maker.
4. Close and cook for 4 minutes.
5. Repeat steps until all the remaining batter has been used.

Nutrition Info: Calories 294Total Fat 26.7g Saturated Fat 12g Cholesterol 133mg Sodium 144mg Potassium 421mgTotal Carbohydrate 11.6g Dietary Fiber 4.5g Protein 6.8g Total Sugars 1.7g

Garlic Chaffles

Servings: 4
Cooking Time: 5 Minutes
Ingredients:

- 1/2 cup mozzarella cheese, shredded
- 1/3 cup cheddar cheese
- 1 large egg
- ½ tbsp. garlic powder
- 1/2 tsp Italian seasoning
- 1/4 tsp baking powder

Directions:

1. Switch on your waffle maker and lightly grease your waffle maker with a brush.
2. Beat the egg with garlic powder, Italian seasoning and baking powder in a small mixing bowl.
3. Add mozzarella cheese and cheddar cheese tothe egg mixture and mix well.
4. Pour half of the chaffles batter into the middle of your waffle iron and close the lid.
5. Cook chaffles for about 2-3 minutes until crispy.
6. Once cooked, remove chaffles from the maker.
7. Sprinkle garlic powder on top and enjoy!

Nutrition Info: Per Serving: Protein: 32% 36 kcal Fat: 61% 69 kcal Carbohydrates: 7% 7 kcal

Zucchini Parmesan Chaffles

Servings: 2
Cooking Time: 14 Minutes
Ingredients:

- 1 cup shredded zucchini
- 1 egg, beaten
- ½ cup finely grated Parmesan cheese
- Salt and freshly ground black pepper to taste

Directions:

1. Preheat the waffle iron.
2. Put all the ingredients in a medium bowl and mix well.
3. Open the iron and add half of the mixture. Close and cook until crispy, 7 minutes.
4. Remove the chaffle onto a plate and make another with the remaining mixture.
5. Cut each chaffle into wedges and serve afterward.

Nutrition Info: Per Serving Calories 138Fats 9.07gCarbs 3.81gNet Carbs 3.71g Protein 10.02g

Layered Cheese Chaffles

Servings: 1
Cooking Time: 5 Minutes
Ingredients:

- 1 organic egg, beaten
- 1/3 cup Cheddar cheese, shredded
- ½ teaspoon ground flaxseed
- ¼ teaspoon organic baking powder
- 2 tablespoons Parmesan cheese, shredded

Directions:

1. Preheat a mini waffle iron and then grease it.
2. In a bowl, place all the ingredients except Parmesan and beat until well combined.
3. Place half the Parmesan cheese in the bottom of preheated waffle iron.
4. Place half of the egg mixture over cheese and top with the remaining Parmesan cheese.
5. Cook for about 3-5 minutes or until golden brown.
6. Serve warm.

Nutrition Info: Per Serving Calories: 264Net Carb: 1.7gFat: 20gSaturated Fat: 11.1g Carbohydrates: 2.1gDietary Fiber: 0.4g Sugar: 0.6g Protein: 18.9g

Pulled Pork Chaffle Sandwiches

Servings: 4
Cooking Time: 28 Minutes

Ingredients:

- 2 eggs, beaten
- 1 cup finely grated cheddar cheese
- ¼ tsp baking powder
- 2 cups cooked and shredded pork
- 1 tbsp sugar-free BBQ sauce
- 2 cups shredded coleslaw mix
- 2 tbsp apple cider vinegar
- ½ tsp salt
- ¼ cup ranch dressing

Directions:

1. Preheat the waffle iron.
2. In a medium bowl, mix the eggs, cheddar cheese, and baking powder.
3. Open the iron and add a quarter of the mixture. Close and cook until crispy, 7 minutes.
4. Transfer the chaffle to a plate and make 3 more chaffles in the same manner.
5. Meanwhile, in another medium bowl, mix the pulled pork with the BBQ sauce until well combined. Set aside.
6. Also, mix the coleslaw mix, apple cider vinegar, salt, and ranch dressing in another medium bowl.
7. When the chaffles are ready, on two pieces, divide the pork and then top with the ranch coleslaw. Cover with the remaining chaffles and insert mini skewers to secure the sandwiches.
8. Enjoy afterward.

Nutrition Info: Calories 374Fats 23.61gCarbs 8.2gNet Carbs 8.2g Protein 28.05g

Mayonnaise Chaffles

Servings: 2
Cooking Time: 10 Minutes

Ingredients:

- 1 large organic egg, beaten
- 1 tablespoon mayonnaise
- 2 tablespoons almond flour
- 1/8 teaspoon organic baking powder
- 1 teaspoon water

Directions:

1. Preheat a mini waffle iron and then grease it.
2. In a medium bowl, place all ingredients and with a fork, mix until well combined.
3. Place half of the mixture into preheated waffle iron and cook for about 4-5 minutes or until golden brown.
4. Repeat with the remaining mixture.
5. Serve warm.

Nutrition Info: Per Serving Calories: 110Net Carb: 2.6gFat: 8.7gSaturated Fat: 1.4g Carbohydrates: 3.4gDietary Fiber: 0.8g Sugar: 0.9g Protein: 3.2g

Egg-free Psyllium Husk Chaffles

Servings: 1
Cooking Time: 4 Minutes

Ingredients:

- 1 ounce Mozzarella cheese, shredded
- 1 tablespoon cream cheese, softened
- 1 tablespoon psyllium husk powder

Directions:

1. Preheat a waffle iron and then grease it.
2. In a blender, place all ingredients and pulse until a slightly crumbly mixture forms.
3. Place the mixture into preheated waffle iron and cook for about 3-4 minutes or until golden brown.
4. Serve warm.

Nutrition Info: Per Serving Calories: 137Net Carb: 1.3gFat: 8.8gSaturated Fat: 5.2g Carbohydrates: 1.3gDietary Fiber: 0g Sugar: 0g Protein: 9.5g

Spicy Shrimp And Chaffles

Servings: 4
Cooking Time: 31 Minutes

Ingredients:

- For the shrimp:
- 1 tbsp olive oil
- 1 lb jumbo shrimp, peeled and deveined
- 1 tbsp Creole seasoning
- Salt to taste
- 2 tbsp hot sauce
- 3 tbsp butter
- 2 tbsp chopped fresh scallions to garnish
- For the chaffles:

- 2 eggs, beaten
- 1 cup finely grated Monterey Jack cheese

Directions:

1. For the shrimp:
2. Heat the olive oil in a medium skillet over medium heat.
3. Season the shrimp with the Creole seasoning and salt. Cook in the oil until pink and opaque on both sides, 2 minutes.
4. Pour in the hot sauce and butter. Mix well until the shrimp is adequately coated in the sauce, 1 minute.
5. Turn the heat off and set aside.
6. For the chaffles:
7. Preheat the waffle iron.
8. In a medium bowl, mix the eggs and Monterey Jack cheese.
9. Open the iron and add a quarter of the mixture. Close and cook until crispy, 7 minutes.
10. Transfer the chaffle to a plate and make 3 more chaffles in the same manner.
11. Cut the chaffles into quarters and place on a plate.
12. Top with the shrimp and garnish with the scallions.
13. Serve warm.

Nutrition Info: Calories 342Fats 19.75gCarbs 2.8gNet Carbs 2.3g Protein 36.01g

Hot Dog Chaffles

Servings: 2
Cooking Time: 14 Minutes

Ingredients:

- 1 egg, beaten
- 1 cup finely grated cheddar cheese
- 2 hot dog sausages, cooked
- Mustard dressing for topping
- 8 pickle slices

Directions:

1. Preheat the waffle iron.
2. In a medium bowl, mix the egg and cheddar cheese.
3. Open the iron and add half of the mixture. Close and cook until crispy, 7 minutes.
4. Transfer the chaffle to a plate and make a second chaffle in the same manner.
5. To serve, top each chaffle with a sausage, swirl the mustard dressing on top, and then divide the pickle slices on top.
6. Enjoy!

Nutrition Info: Calories 231Fats 18.29gCarbs 2.8gNet Carbs 2.6g Protein 13.39g

Colby Jack Slices Chaffles

Servings: 1
Cooking Time: 6 Minutes

Ingredients:

- 2 ounces Colby Jack cheese, cut into thin triangle slices
- 1 large organic egg, beaten

Directions:

1. Preheat a waffle iron and then grease it.
2. Arrange 1 thin layer of cheese slices in the bottom of preheated waffle iron.
3. Place the beaten egg on top of the cheese.
4. Now, arrange another layer of cheese slices on top to cover evenly.
5. Cook for about 5-6 minutes or until golden brown.
6. Serve warm.

Nutrition Info: Per Serving Calories: 292Net Carb: 2.4gFat: 23gSaturated Fat: 13.6g Carbohydrates: 2.4gDietary Fiber: 0g Sugar: 0.4g Protein: 18.3g

Keto Cocoa Chaffles

Servings: 2
Cooking Time: 5 Minutes

Ingredients:

- 1 large egg
- 1/2 cup shredded cheddar cheese
- 1 tbsp. cocoa powder
- 2 tbsps. almond flour

Directions:

1. Preheat your round waffle maker on medium-high heat.
2. Mix together egg, cheese, almond flour, cocoa powder and vanilla in a small mixing bowl.
3. Pour chaffles mixture into the center of the waffle iron.
4. Close the waffle maker and let cook for 3-5 minutes or until waffle is golden brown and set.
5. Carefully remove chaffles from the waffle maker.
6. Serve hot and enjoy!

Nutrition Info: Per Serving: Protein: 20% 49 kcal Fat: 73% 183 kcal Carbohydrates: 7% 17 kcal

Guacamole Chaffle Bites

Servings: 2
Cooking Time: 14 Minutes

Ingredients:

- 1 large turnip, cooked and mashed
- 2 bacon slices, cooked and finely chopped
- ½ cup finely grated Monterey Jack cheese
- 1 egg, beaten
- 1 cup guacamole for topping

Directions:

1. Preheat the waffle iron.
2. Mix all the ingredients except for the guacamole in a medium bowl.
3. Open the iron and add half of the mixture. Close and cook for 4 minutes. Open the lid, flip the chaffle and cook further until golden brown and crispy, 3 minutes.
4. Remove the chaffle onto a plate and make another in the same manner.
5. Cut each chaffle into wedges, top with the guacamole and serve afterward.

Nutrition Info: Per Serving Calories 311Fats 22.52gCarbs 8.29gNet Carbs 5.79g Protein 13.62g

Blue Cheese Chaffle Bites

Servings: 2
Cooking Time: 14 Minutes
Ingredients:
- 1 egg, beaten
- ½ cup finely grated Parmesan cheese
- ¼ cup crumbled blue cheese
- 1 tsp erythritol

Directions:
1. Preheat the waffle iron.
2. Mix all the ingredients in a bowl.
3. Open the iron and add half of the mixture. Close and cook until crispy, 7 minutes.
4. Remove the chaffle onto a plate and make another with the remaining mixture.
5. Cut each chaffle into wedges and serve afterward.

Nutrition Info: Per Serving Calories 196Fats 13.91gCarbs 4.03gNet Carbs 4.03g Protein 13.48g

Simple Chaffle Toast

Servings: 2
Cooking Time: 5 Minutes
Ingredients:
- 1 large egg
- 1/2 cup shredded cheddar cheese
- FOR TOPPING
- 1 egg
- 3-4 spinach leaves
- ¼ cup boil and shredded chicken

Directions:
1. Preheat your square waffle maker on medium-high heat.
2. Mix together egg and cheese in a bowl and make two chaffles in a chaffle maker
3. Once chaffle are cooked, carefully remove them from the maker.
4. Serve with spinach, boiled chicken, and fried egg.
5. Serve hot and enjoy!

Nutrition Info: Per Serving: Protein: 39% 99 kcal Fat: 60% 153 kcal Carbohydrates: 1% 3 kcal

Egg-free Almond Flour Chaffles

Servings: 2
Cooking Time: 10 Minutes
Ingredients:
- 2 tablespoons cream cheese, softened
- 1 cup mozzarella cheese, shredded
- 2 tablespoons almond flour
- 1 teaspoon organic baking powder

Directions:
1. Preheat a mini waffle iron and then grease it.
2. In a medium bowl, place all ingredients and with a fork, mix until well combined.

3. Place half of the mixture into preheated waffle iron and cook for about 4-5 minutes or until golden brown.
4. Repeat with the remaining mixture.
5. Serve warm.

Nutrition Info: Per Serving Calories: 77Net Carb: 2.4gFat: 9.8gSaturated Fat: 4g Carbohydrates: 3.2gDietary Fiber: 0.8g Sugar: 0.3g Protein: 4.8g

Chaffled Brownie Sundae

Servings: 4
Cooking Time: 30 Minutes

Ingredients:

- For the chaffles:
- 2 eggs, beaten
- 1 tbsp unsweetened cocoa powder
- 1 tbsp erythritol
- 1 cup finely grated mozzarella cheese
- For the topping:
- 3 tbsp unsweetened chocolate, chopped
- 3 tbsp unsalted butter
- ½ cup swerve sugar
- Low-carb ice cream for topping
- 1 cup whipped cream for topping
- 3 tbsp sugar-free caramel sauce

Directions:

1. For the chaffles:
2. Preheat the waffle iron.
3. Meanwhile, in a medium bowl, mix all the ingredients for the chaffles.
4. Open the iron, pour in a quarter of the mixture, cover, and cook until crispy, 7 minutes.
5. Remove the chaffle onto a plate and make 3 more with the remaining batter.
6. Plate and set aside.
7. For the topping:
8. Meanwhile, melt the chocolate and butter in a medium saucepan with occasional stirring, 2 minutes.
9. To Servings:
10. Divide the chaffles into wedges and top with the ice cream, whipped cream, and swirl the chocolate sauce and caramel sauce on top.
11. Serve immediately.

Nutrition Info: Calories 165Fats 11.39gCarbs 3.81gNet Carbs 2.91g Protein 12.79g

KETO CHAFFLE RECIPES VARIATIONS

Garlic Bread Chaffles

Servings: 2
Cooking Time: 11 Minutes
Ingredients:

- 1/2 cup shredded Mozzarella cheese
- 1 egg
- 1/2 tsp basil
- 1/4 tsp garlic powder
- 1 tbsp almond flour
- 1 tbsp butter
- 1/4 tsp garlic powder
- 1/4 cup shredded mozzarella cheese

Directions:

1. Heat up your Dash mini waffle maker.
2. In a small bowl, mix the egg, 1/2 tsp basil, 1/4 tsp garlic powder, 1 tablespoon almond flour and 1/2 cup Mozzarella Cheese.
3. Add 1/2 of the batter into your mini waffle maker and cook for 4 minutes. If they are still a bit uncooked, leave it cooking for another 2 minutes. Then cook the rest of the batter to make a second chaffle.
4. In a small bowl, add 1 tablespoon butter and 1/4 tsp garlic powder and melt in the microwave. It will take about 25 seconds or so, depending on your microwave.
5. Place the chaffles on a baking sheet and use a rubber brush to spread the butter and garlic mixture on top.
6. Add 1/8th a cup of cheese on top of each chaffle.
7. Put chaffles in the oven or a toaster oven at 400 degrees and cook until the cheese is melted.

Nutrition Info: (Per Serving):Calories: 231kcal ;Carbohydrates:2g ;Protein: 13g;Fat: 19g ;Saturated Fat:10g ;Cholesterol:130mg ;Sodium:346mg ;Potassium: 52mg ;Fiber: 1g ;Sugar: 1g ;Vitamin A: 580IU ;Calcium: 232mg ;Iron: 1mg

Basic Keto Low Carb Chaffle Recipe

Servings: 1
Cooking Time: 8 Minutes
Ingredients:

- 1 egg
- 1/2 cup cheddar cheese, shredded

Directions:

1. Turn waffle maker on or plug it in so that it heats and grease both sides.
2. In a small bowl, crack an egg, then add the 1/2 cup cheddar cheese and stir to combine.
3. Pour 1/2 of the batter in the waffle maker and close the top.
4. Cook for 3-4 minutes or until it reaches desired doneness.
5. Carefully remove from waffle maker and set aside for 2-3 minutes to give it time to crisp.
6. Follow the instructions again to make the second chaffle.

Nutrition Info: (Per Serving):Calories: 291kcal;Carbohydrates:1g;Protein: 20g;Fat: 23g;Saturated Fat:13g;Cholesterol:223mg;Sodium:413mg;Potassium: 116mg;Sugar: 1g;Vitamin A: 804IU;Calcium: 432mg;Iron: 1mg

Chocolate Chip Chaffles

Servings: 2
Cooking Time: 8 Minutes
Ingredients:
- 1/2 cup shredded mozzarella cheese
- 1 tbsp almond flour
- 1 egg
- 1/4 tsp cinnamon
- 1/2 tbsp Granulated Swerve
- 2 tablespoon low carb chocolate chips like Lily's chocolate chips

Directions:
1. Plug in your waffle maker.
2. In a small bowl, mix the mozzarella cheese, almond flour, egg, cinnamon, swerve, and chocolate chips.
3. Add half the keto chocolate chip Chaffle batter to the Dish Mini waffle maker at a time. Cook chaffle batter in the waffle maker for 4 minutes.
4. When the first one is completely done cooking cook the second one.
5. Let each chaffle sit for 1-2 minutes on a plate to firm up. Enjoy alone, sprinkled with powdered sugar, or whipped cream on top.

Nutrition Info: (Per Serving):Calories: 136kcal ;Carbohydrates:2g ;Protein: 10g;Fat: 10g ;Saturated Fat:5g ;Cholesterol:104mg ;Sodium:207mg ;Potassium: 52mg ;Fiber: 1g ;Sugar: 1g ;Vitamin A: 308IU ;Calcium: 161mg ;Iron: 1mg

Cinnamon Roll Keto Chaffles

Servings: 3
Cooking Time: 10 Minutes
Ingredients:
- Cinnamon Roll Chaffle
- 1/2 cup mozzarella cheese
- 1 tablespoon almond flour
- 1/4 tsp baking powder
- 1 egg
- 1 tsp cinnamon
- 1 tsp Granulated Swerve
- Cinnamon roll swirl
- 1 tbsp butter
- 1 tsp cinnamon
- 2 tsp confectioners swerve
- Keto Cinnamon Roll Glaze
- 1 tablespoon butter
- 1 tablespoon cream cheese
- 1/4 tsp vanilla extract
- 2 tsp swerve confectioners

Directions:

1. Plug in your Mini Dash Waffle maker and let it heat up.
2. In a small bowl mix the mozzarella cheese, almond flour, baking powder, egg, 1 teaspoon cinnamon, and 1 teaspoon swerve granulated and set aside.
3. In another small bowl, add a tablespoon of butter, 1 teaspoon cinnamon, and 2 teaspoons of swerve confectioners sweetener.
4. Microwave for 15 seconds and mix well.
5. Spray the waffle maker with nonstick spray and add 1/3 of the batter to your waffle maker. Swirl in 1/3 of the cinnamon, swerve, and butter mixture onto the top of it. Close the waffle maker and let cook for 3-4 minutes.
6. When the first cinnamon roll chaffle is done, make the second and then make the third.
7. While the third chaffle is cooking place 1 tablespoon butter and 1 tablespoon of cream cheese in a small bowl. Heat in the microwave for 10-15 seconds. Start at 10, and if the cream cheese is not soft enough to mix with the butter heat for an additional 5 seconds.
8. Add the vanilla extract, and the swerve confectioners sweetener to the butter and cream cheese and mix well using a whisk.
9. Drizzle keto cream cheese glaze on top of chaffle.

Nutrition Info: (Per Serving):Calories: 180kcal;Carbohydrates:3g;Protein: 7g;Fat: 16g;Saturated Fat:9g;Cholesterol:95mg;Sodium:221mg;Potassium: 77mg;Fiber: 1g;Sugar: 1g;Vitamin A: 505IU;Calcium: 148mg;Iron: 1mg

Maple Pumpkin Keto Chaffle Recipe

Servings: 2
Cooking Time: 16 Minutes

Ingredients:

- 2 eggs
- 3/4 tsp baking powder
- 2 tsp pumpkin puree (100% pumpkin)
- 3/4 tsp pumpkin pie spice
- 4 tsp heavy whipping cream
- 2 tsp Lakanto Sugar-Free Maple Syrup
- 1 tsp coconut flour
- 1/2 cup mozzarella cheese, shredded
- 1/2 tsp vanilla
- Pinch of salt

Directions:

1. Turn on chaffle maker.
2. In a small bowl, combine all ingredients.
3. Cover the dash mini waffle maker with 1/4 of the batter and cook for 3-4 minutes.
4. Repeat 3 more times until you have made 4 Maple Syrup Pumpkin Keto Waffles (Chaffles).
5. Serve with sugar-free maple syrup or keto ice cream.

Nutrition Info: (Per Serving):Calories: 201kcal;Carbohydrates:4g;Protein: 12g;Fat: 15g;Saturated Fat:8g;Cholesterol:200mg;Sodium:249mg;Potassium: 271mg;Fiber: 1g;Sugar: 1g;Vitamin A: 1341IU;Calcium: 254mg;Iron: 1mg

Keto Blueberry Chaffle

Servings: 5
Cooking Time: 15 Minutes
Ingredients:

- 1 cup of mozzarella cheese
- 2 tablespoons almond flour
- 1 tsp baking powder
- 2 eggs
- 1 tsp cinnamon
- 2 tsp of Swerve
- 3 tablespoon blueberries

Directions:

1. Heat up your Dash mini waffle maker.
2. In a mixing bowl, add the mozzarella cheese, almond flour, baking powder, eggs, cinnamon, swerve, and blueberries. Mix well, so all the ingredients are mixed together.
3. Spray your mini waffle maker with nonstick cooking spray.
4. Add in a little bit less than 1/4 a cup of blueberry keto waffle batter.
5. Close the lid and cook the chaffle for 3-5 minutes. Check it at the 3-minute mark to see if it is crispy and brown. If it is not or it sticks to the top of the waffle machine, close the lid and cook for 1-2 minutes longer.
6. Serve with a sprinkle of swerve confectioners sugar or keto syrup.

Nutrition Info: (Per Serving):Calories: 116kcal;Carbohydrates:3g;Protein: 8g;Fat: 8g;Saturated Fat:4g;Cholesterol:83mg;Sodium:166mg;Potassium: 142mg;Fiber: 1g;Sugar: 1g;Vitamin A: 246IU;Vitamin C: 1mg;Calcium: 177mg;Iron: 1mg

Peanut Butter Chocolate Chip Chaffle

Servings: 2
Cooking Time: 8 Minutes
Ingredients:

- 1 egg.
- 1/4 cup shredded mozzarella cheese
- 2 tablespoons creamy Peanut Butter.
- 1 tablespoon Almond Flour.
- 1 tablespoon Granulated Swerve.
- 1 teaspoon Vanilla extract.
- 1 tablespoon low carb chocolate chips.

Directions:

1. Plug in your waffle maker.
2. In a small bowl, mix the peanut butter and egg. Make sure you mix it well, so all the peanut butter is mixed with the egg.
3. Next, add in the mozzarella cheese, almond flour, swerve and chocolate chips and mix well.
4. Add half the keto peanut butter chocolate chip Chaffle mix to the Dish Mini waffle maker at a time. Cook chaffle batter in the waffle maker for 4 minutes.
5. When the first one is completely done cooking cook the second one.
6. Enjoy with some swerve confectioners sweetener or whipped cream on top.

Nutrition Info: (Per Serving):Calories: 193kcal ;Carbohydrates:5g ;Protein: 11g;Fat: 15g ;Saturated Fat:4g ;Cholesterol:93mg ;Sodium:193mg ;Potassium: 134mg ;Fiber: 1g ;Sugar: 2g ;Vitamin A: 213IU ;Calcium: 97mg ;Iron: 1mg

Best Keto Pizza Chaffle

Servings: 2
Cooking Time: 15 Minutes
Ingredients:
- 1 tsp coconut flour
- 1 egg white
- 1/2 cup mozzarella cheese, shredded
- `1 tsp cream cheese, softened
- 1/4 tsp baking powder
- 1/8 tsp Italian seasoning
- 1/8 tsp garlic powder
- pinch of salt
- 3 tsp low carb marinara sauce
- 1/2 cup mozzarella cheese
- 6 pepperonis cut in half
- 1 tbsp parmesan cheese, shredded
- 1/4 tsp basil seasoning

Directions:
1. Preheat oven to 400 degrees. Turn waffle maker on or plug it in so that it gets hot.
2. In a small bowl, add coconut flour, egg white, mozzarella cheese, softened cream cheese, baking powder, garlic powder, Italian seasonings, and a pinch of salt.
3. Pour 1/2 of the batter in the waffle maker, close the top, and cook for 3-4 minutes or until chaffle reaches desired doneness.
4. Carefully remove chaffle from the waffle maker, then follow the same instructions to make the second chaffle.
5. Top each chaffle with tomato sauce (I used 1 1/2 tsp per), pepperoni, mozzarella cheese, and parmesan cheese.
6. Place in the oven on a baking sheet (or straight on the baking rack) on the top shelf of the oven for 5-6 minutes. Then turn the oven to broil so that the cheese begins to bubble and brown. Keep a close eye as it can burn quickly. I broiled my pizza chaffle for approx 1 min and 30 seconds.
7. Remove from oven and sprinkle basil on top.
8. Enjoy!
9. Note:
10. The nutritional information provided is for one of the keto Pizza Chaffle so that each person could choose how much they wanted to eat to fit their hunger levels and health goals.

Nutrition Info: (Per Serving):Calories: 241kcal ;Carbohydrates:4g ;Protein: 17g;Fat: 18g ;Saturated Fat:10g ;Cholesterol:49mg ;Sodium:430mg ;Potassium: 130mg ;Fiber: 1g ;Sugar: 1g ;Vitamin A: 412IU ;Calcium: 339mg ;Iron: 1mg

Mouthwatering Blueberry Chaffles

Servings: 2
Cooking Time: 8 Minutes
Ingredients:

- 1 egg
- 1/3 cup mozzarella cheese, shredded
- 1 tbsp blueberries
- 1 tsp cream cheese
- 1 tsp coconut flour
- 1/4 tsp baking powder
- 1/4 tsp vanilla extract
- 2 squirts liquid Pyure Sweetener (can substitute 3/4 tsp other sweeteners such as Monkfruit powdered)
- 1/4 tsp cinnamon
- Pinch of salt

Directions:

1. Turn on waffle or chaffle maker. Grease lightly or use a cooking spray.
2. In a small bowl, combine all ingredients except the blueberries
3. Cover the dash mini waffle maker with 1/2 of the batter then sprinkle a couple of blueberries on top. Close the mini waffle maker and cook for 4 minutes. Remove the chaffle from the waffle maker carefully,
4. Repeat the steps above.
5. Serve with sugar-free maple syrup, whipped cream, or keto ice cream.

Nutrition Info: (Per Serving):Calories: 113kcal ;Carbohydrates:3g ;Protein: 7g;Fat: 7g ;Saturated Fat:4g ;Cholesterol:99mg ;Sodium:162mg ;Potassium: 93mg ;Fiber: 1g ;Sugar: 1g ;Vitamin A: 278IU ;Vitamin C: 1mg ;Calcium: 134mg ;Iron: 1mg

Cheesy Garlic Chaffle Bread Recipe

Servings: 2
Cooking Time: 14 Minutes
Ingredients:

- 1 egg
- 1/2 cup mozzarella cheese, shredded
- 1 tbsp parmesan cheese
- 3/4 tsp coconut flour
- 1/4 tsp baking powder
- 1/8 tsp Italian Seasoning
- Pinch of salt
- 1 tbsp butter, melted
- 1/4 tsp garlic powder
- 1/2 cup mozzarella cheese, shredded
- 1/4 tsp basil seasoning

Directions:

1. Preheat oven to 400 degrees. Plug the Dash Mini Waffle Maker in the wall and allow it to get hot. Lightly grease waffle maker.
2. Combine the first 7 ingredients in a small bowl and stir well to combine.

3. Spoon half of the batter on the waffle maker and close — Cook for 3-4 minutes or until golden brown.
4. Remove the chaffle bread carefully from the Dash Mini Waffle Maker, then repeat for the rest of the batter.
5. In a small bowl, melt the butter and add garlic powder.
6. Cut each chaffle in half (or thirds), and place on a baking sheet, then brush the tops with the garlic butter mixture.
7. Top with mozzarella cheese and pop in the oven for 4 -5 minutes.
8. Turn oven to broil and move the baking pan to the top shelf for 1-2 minutes so that the cheese begins to bubble and turn golden brown. Watch very carefully, as it can burn quickly on broil. (check every 30 seconds)
9. Remove from oven and sprinkle basil seasoning on top. Enjoy!

Nutrition Info: (Per Serving):Calories: 270kcal ;Carbohydrates:3g ;Protein: 16g;Fat: 21g ;Saturated Fat:12g;Fiber: 1g ;Sugar: 1g

Fudgy Chocolate Chaffles

Servings: 2
Cooking Time: 8 Minutes

Ingredients:

- 1 egg
- 2 tbsp mozzarella cheese, shredded
- 2 tbsp cocoa
- 2 tbsp Lakanto monk fruit powdered
- 1 tsp coconut flour
- 1 tsp heavy whipping cream
- 1/4 tsp baking powder
- 1/4 tsp vanilla extract
- pinch of salt

Directions:

1. Turn on waffle or chaffle maker. I use the Dash Mini Waffle Maker. Grease lightly or use a cooking spray.
2. In a small bowl, combine all ingredients.
3. Cover the dash mini waffle maker with 1/2 of the batter. Close the mini waffle maker and cook for 4 minutes. Remove the chaffle from the waffle maker carefully as it is very hot.
4. Repeat the steps above.
5. Serve with sugar-free strawberry ice cream or sugar-free whipped topping.
6. Note:
7. The nutritional information does not include the Lakanto Monkfruit powdered sugar as most subtract to calculate net carbs. The nutritional info is based on one chaffle Per Serving.
8. The nutritional information is provided for the fudgy chocolate chaffle recipe only.

Nutrition Info: (Per Serving):Calories: 109kcal ;Carbohydrates:5g ;Protein: 7g;Fat: 7g ;Saturated Fat:4g ;Cholesterol:97mg ;Sodium:132mg ;Potassium: 176mg ;Fiber: 3g ;Sugar: 1g ;Vitamin A: 255IU ;Calcium: 121mg ;Iron: 1mg

Mini Keto Pizza Chaffle Recipe

Servings: 1
Cooking Time: 10 Minutes
Ingredients:

- 1/2 cup Shredded Mozzarella cheese
- 1 tablespoon almond flour
- 1/2 tsp baking powder
- 1 egg
- 1/4 tsp garlic powder
- 1/4 tsp basil
- 2 tablespoons low carb pasta sauce
- 2 tablespoons mozzarella cheese

Directions:

1. While the waffle maker is heating up, in a bowl mix mozzarella cheese, baking powder, garlic, basil, egg, and almond flour.
2. Pour 1/2 the mixture into your mini waffle maker.
3. Cook for 3-5 minutes until your pizza waffle is completely cooked. If you check it and the waffle sticks to the waffle maker, let it cook for another minute or two.
4. Next, put the remainder of the pizza crust mix into the waffle maker and cook it.
5. Once both pizza crusts are cooked, place them on the baking sheet of your toaster oven.
6. Put 1 tablespoon of low carb pasta sauce on top of each pizza crust.
7. Sprinkle 1 tablespoon of shredded mozzarella cheese on top of each one.
8. Bake at 350 degrees in the toaster oven for roughly 5 minutes, just until the cheese is melted.

Nutrition Info: (Per Serving):Calories: 195kcal;Carbohydrates:4g;Protein: 13g;Fat: 14g;Saturated Fat:6g;Cholesterol:116mg;Sodium:301mg;Potassium: 178mg;Fiber: 1g;Sugar: 1g;Vitamin A: 408IU;Calcium: 290mg;Iron: 1mg

Pumpkin Chocolate Chip Chaffles

Servings: 3
Cooking Time: 12 Minutes
Ingredients:

- 1/2 cup shredded mozzarella cheese
- 4 teaspoons pumpkin puree
- 1 egg
- 2 tablespoons granulated Swerve
- 1/4 tsp pumpkin pie spice
- 4 teaspoons sugar-free chocolate chips
- 1 tablespoon almond flour

Directions:

1. Plug in your waffle maker.
2. In a small bowl, mix the pumpkin puree and egg. Make sure you mix it well, so all the pumpkin is mixed with the egg.
3. Next, add in the mozzarella cheese, almond flour, swerve and add pumpkin spice and mix well.
4. Then add in your sugar-free chocolate chips

5. Add half the keto pumpkin pie Chaffle mix to the Dish Mini waffle maker at a time. Cook chaffle batter in the waffle maker for 4 minutes.
6. Do not open before the 4 minutes is up. It is very important that you do not open the waffle maker before the 4-minute mark. After that you can open it to check it and make sure it is cooked all the way, but with these chaffles keeping the lid closed the whole time is very important.
7. When the first one is completely done cooking cook the second one.
8. Enjoy with some swerve confectioners sweetener or whipped cream on top.

Nutrition Info: (Per Serving):Calories: 93kcal ;Carbohydrates:2g ;Protein: 7g;Fat: 7g ;Saturated Fat:3g ;Cholesterol:69mg ;Sodium:138mg ;Potassium: 48mg ;Fiber: 1g ;Sugar: 1g ;Vitamin A: 1228IU ;Calcium: 107mg ;Iron: 1mg

Chocolate Chip Chaffle Keto Recipe

Servings: 1
Cooking Time: 8 Minutes

Ingredients:

- 1 egg
- 1 tbsp heavy whipping cream
- 1/2 tsp coconut flour
- 1 3/4 tsp Lakanto monk fruit golden can use more or less to adjust sweetness
- 1/4 tsp baking powder
- pinch of salt
- 1 tbsp Lily's Chocolate Chips

Directions:

1. Turn on the waffle maker so that it heats up.
2. In a small bowl, combine all ingredients except the chocolate chips and stir well until combined.
3. Grease waffle maker, then pour half of the batter onto the bottom plate of the waffle maker. Sprinkle a few chocolate chips on top and then close.
4. Cook for 3-4 minutes or until the chocolate chip chaffle dessert is golden brown, then remove from waffle maker with a fork, being careful not to burn your fingers.
5. Repeat with the rest of the batter.
6. Let chaffle sit for a few minutes so that it begins to crisp. If desired, serve with sugar-free whipped topping.

Nutrition Info: (Per Serving):Calories: 146kcal;Carbohydrates:7g;Protein: 6g;Fat: 10g;Saturated Fat:7g;Fiber: 3g;Sugar: 1g

SWEET CHAFFLES RECIPES

Mocha Chaffles

Servings: 3
Cooking Time: 9 Minutes
Ingredients:

- 1 organic egg, beaten
- 1 tablespoon cacao powder
- 1 tablespoon Erythritol
- ¼ teaspoon organic baking powder
- 2 tablespoons cream cheese, softened
- 1 tablespoon mayonnaise
- ¼ teaspoon instant coffee powder
- Pinch of salt
- 1 teaspoon organic vanilla extract

Directions:

1. Preheat a mini waffle iron and then grease it.
2. In a medium bowl, place all ingredients and with a fork, mix until well combined.
3. Place 1/3 of the mixture into preheated waffle iron and cook for about 2½-3 minutes or until golden brown.
4. Repeat with the remaining mixture.
5. Serve warm.

Nutrition Info: Per Serving Calories: 83Net Carb: 1gFat: 7.5gSaturated Fat: 4.6g Carbohydrates: 1.5gDietary Fiber: 0.5g Sugar: 0.3g Protein: 2.7g

Chocolate Chips Lemon Chaffles

Servings: 4
Cooking Time: 8 Minutes
Ingredients:

- 2 organic eggs
- ½ cup Mozzarella cheese, shredded
- ¾ teaspoon organic lemon extract
- ½ teaspoon organic vanilla extract
- 2 teaspoons Erythritol
- ½ teaspoon psyllium husk powder
- Pinch of salt
- 1 tablespoon 70% dark chocolate chips
- ¼ teaspoon lemon zest, grated finely

Directions:

1. Preheat a mini waffle iron and then grease it.
2. In a bowl, place all ingredients except chocolate chips and lemon zest and beat until well combined.
3. Gently, fold in the chocolate chips and lemon zest.
4. Place ¼ of the mixture into preheated waffle iron and cook for about 4 minutes or until golden brown.
5. Repeat with the remaining mixture.

6. Serve warm.

Nutrition Info: Per Serving Calories: 71Net Carb: 1gFat: 4.8gSaturated Fat: 2.3g Carbohydrates: 1.5gDietary Fiber: 0.5g Sugar: 0.3g Protein: 4.3g

Vanilla Chaffle

Servings: 2

Cooking Time: 8 Minutes

Ingredients:

- 2 tbsp butter, softened
- 2 oz cream cheese, softened
- 2 eggs
- ¼ cup almond flour
- 2 tbsp coconut flour
- 1 tsp baking powder
- 1 tsp vanilla extract
- ¼ cup confectioners
- Pinch of pink salt

Directions:

1. Preheat the waffle maker and spray with non-stick cooking spray.
2. Melt the butter and set aside for a minute to cool.
3. Add the eggs into the melted butter and whisk until creamy.
4. Pour in the sweetener, vanilla, extract, and salt. Blend properly.
5. Next add the coconut flour, almond flour, and baking powder. Mix well.
6. Pour into the waffle maker and cook for 4 minutes.
7. Repeat the process with the remaining batter.
8. Remove and set aside to cool.
9. Enjoy.

Nutrition Info: Calories Per Serving 202 Kcal; Fats: 27 g ; Carbs: 9 g ; Protein: 23 g

Butter & Cream Cheese Chaffles

Servings: 4

Cooking Time: 16 Minutes

Ingredients:

- 2 tablespoons butter, melted and cooled
- 2 large organic eggs
- 2 ounces cream cheese, softened
- ¼ cup powdered erythritol
- 1½ teaspoons organic vanilla extract
- Pinch of salt
- ¼ cup almond flour
- 2 tablespoons coconut flour
- 1 teaspoon organic baking powder

Directions:

1. Preheat a mini waffle iron and then grease it.
2. In a bowl, add the butter and eggs and beat until creamy.

3. Add the cream cheese, erythritol, vanilla extract, and salt, and beat until well combined.
4. Add the flours and baking powder and beat until well combined.
5. Place ¼ of the mixture into preheated waffle iron and cook for about 4 minutes.
6. Repeat with the remaining mixture.
7. Serve warm.

Nutrition Info: Calories 217 Net Carbs 3.3 g Total Fat 18 g Saturated Fat 8.8 g Cholesterol 124 mg Sodium 173 mg Total Carbs 6.6 g Fiber 3.3 g Sugar 1.2 g Protein 5.3 g

Chocolate Peanut Butter Chaffles

Servings: 2
Cooking Time: 8 Minutes

Ingredients:

- 1 organic egg, beaten
- ¼ cup mozzarella cheese, shredded
- 2 tablespoons creamy peanut butter
- 1 tablespoon almond flour
- 1 tablespoon granulated erythritol
- 1 teaspoon organic vanilla extract
- 1 tablespoon 70% dark chocolate chips

Directions:

1. Preheat a mini waffle iron and then grease it.
2. In a bowl, add all ingredients except chocolate and beat until well combined.Gently, fold in the chocolate chips.
3. Place half of the mixture into preheated waffle iron and cook for about 4 minutes.
4. Repeat with the remaining mixture.
5. Serve warm.

Nutrition Info: Calories 214 Net Carbs 4.1 g Total Fat 16.8 g Saturated Fat 5.4 g Cholesterol 84 mg Sodium 128 mg Total Carbs 6.4 g Fiber 2.3 g Sugar 2.1 g Protein 8.8 g

Simple Mozzarella Chaffles

Servings: 2
Cooking Time: 8 Minutes

Ingredients:

- ½ cup mozzarella cheese, shredded
- 1 large organic egg
- 2 tablespoons blanched almond flour
- ¼ teaspoon organic baking powder
- 2-3 drops liquid stevia

Directions:

1. Preheat a mini waffle iron and then grease it.
2. In a medium bowl, put all ingredients and with a fork, mix until well combined.Place half of the mixture into preheated waffle iron and cook for about 3-4 minutes.
3. Repeat with the remaining mixture.
4. Serve warm.

Nutrition Info: Calories 98 Net Carbs 1.4 g Total Fat 7.1 g Saturated Fat 1.8 g Cholesterol 97 mg Sodium 81 mg Total Carbs 2.2 g Fiber 0.8 g Sugar 0.2 g Protein 6.7 g

Basic Keto Chaffles

Servings: 2
Cooking Time: 5 Minutes

Ingredients:

- 1 egg
- ½ cup shredded Cheddar cheese

Directions:

1. Turn on waffle maker to heat and oil it with cooking spray.
2. Whisk egg in a bowl until well beaten.
3. Add cheese to the egg and stir well to combine.
4. Pour ½ batter into the waffle maker and close the top. Cook for 3-5 minutes.
5. Transfer chaffle to a plate and set aside for 2-3 minutes to crisp up.
6. Repeat for remaining batter.

Nutrition Info: Carbs: 1 g ;Fat: 12 g ;Protein: 9 g ;Calories: 150

Oreo Chaffles

Servings: 2
Cooking Time: 5 Minutes

Ingredients:

- Chocolate Chaffle:
- 2 eggs
- 2 tbsp cocoa, unsweetened
- 2 tbsp sweetener
- 2 tbsp heavy cream
- 2 tsp coconut flour
- 1/2 tsp baking powder
- 1 tsp vanilla
- Filling:
- Whipped cream
- Pour half of the mixture into the waffle iron. Cook for 5 minutes.
- Once ready, carefully remove and repeat with the remaining chaffle mixture.
- Allow the cooked chaffles to sit for 3 minutes.
- Once they have cooled, spread the whipped cream on the chaffles and stack them cream side facing down to form a sandwich.
- Slice into halves and enjoy.

Directions:

1. Preheat the mini waffle maker.
2. In a small bowl, add all chaffle

Nutrition Info: Calories Per Serving 390 Kcal; Fats: 40 g ; Carbs: 3 g ; Protein: 10 g

Spiced Pumpkin Chaffles

Servings: 2
Cooking Time: 8 Minutes
Ingredients:

- 1 organic egg, beaten
- ½ cup Mozzarella cheese, shredded
- 1 tablespoon sugar-free canned solid pumpkin
- ¼ teaspoon ground cinnamon
- Pinch of ground cloves
- Pinch of ground nutmeg
- Pinch of ground ginger

Directions:

1. Preheat a mini waffle iron and then grease it.
2. In a medium bowl, place all ingredients and with a fork, mix until well combined.
3. Place half of the mixture into preheated waffle iron and cook for about 3-4 minutes or until golden brown.
4. Repeat with the remaining mixture.
5. Serve warm.

Nutrition Info: Per Serving Calories: 56Net Carb: 1gFat: 3.5gSaturated Fat: 1.5g Carbohydrates: 1.4gDietary Fiber: 0.4g Sugar: 0.5g Protein: 4.9g

Walnut Pumpkin Chaffles

Servings: 2
Cooking Time: 10 Minutes
Ingredients:

- 1 organic egg, beaten
- ½ cup Mozzarella cheese, shredded
- 2 tablespoons almond flour
- 1 tablespoon sugar-free pumpkin puree
- 1 teaspoon Erythritol
- ¼ teaspoon ground cinnamon
- 2 tablespoons walnuts, toasted and chopped

Directions:

1. Preheat a mini waffle iron and then grease it.
2. In a bowl, place all ingredients except walnuts and beat until well combined.
3. Fold in the walnuts.
4. Place half of the mixture into preheated waffle iron and cook for about 5 minutes or until golden brown.
5. Repeat with the remaining mixture.
6. Serve warm.

Nutrition Info: Per Serving Calories: 148Net Carb: 1.6gFat: 11.8gSaturated Fat: 2g Carbohydrates: 3.3gDietary Fiber: 1.7g Sugar: 0.8g Protein: 6.7g

Chocolate Whipping Cream Chaffles

Servings: 2

Cooking Time: 8 Minutes

Ingredients:

- 1 tablespoon almond flour
- 2 tablespoons cacao powder
- 2 tablespoons granulated Erythritol
- ¼ teaspoon organic baking powder
- 1 organic egg
- 1 tablespoon heavy whipping cream
- ¼ teaspoon organic vanilla extract
- 1/8 teaspoon organic almond extract

Directions:

1. Preheat a mini waffle iron and then grease it.
2. In a bowl, place all ingredients and beat until well combined.
3. Place half of the mixture into preheated waffle iron and cook for about 4 minutes or until golden brown.
4. Repeat with the remaining mixture.
5. Serve warm.

Nutrition Info: Per Serving Calories: 94Net Carb: 2gFat: 7.9gSaturated Fat: 3.2g Carbohydrates: 3.9gDietary Fiber: 1.9g Sugar: 0.4g Protein: 3.9g

Cinnamon Chaffles

Servings: 2

Cooking Time: 8 Minutes

Ingredients:

- 1 large organic egg, beaten
- ¾ cup mozzarella cheese, shredded
- ½ tablespoon unsalted butter, melted
- 2 tablespoons blanched almond flour
- 2 tablespoons erythritol
- ½ teaspoon ground cinnamon
- ½ teaspoon Psyllium husk powder
- ¼ teaspoon organic baking powder
- ½ teaspoon organic vanilla extract
- Topping
- 1 teaspoon powdered Erythritol
- ¾ teaspoon ground cinnamon

Directions:

1. Preheat a waffle iron and then grease it.
2. For chaffles: In a medium bowl, put all ingredients and with a fork, mix until well combined.
3. Place half of the mixture into preheated waffle iron and cook for about 3–5 minutes.
4. Repeat with the remaining mixture.
5. Meanwhile, for topping: in a small bowl, mix together the erythritol and cinnamon.
6. Place the chaffles onto serving plates and set aside to cool slightly.
7. Sprinkle with the cinnamon mixture and serve immediately.

Nutrition Info: Calories 142 Net Carbs 2.1 g Total Fat 10.6 g Saturated Fat 4 g Cholesterol 106 mg Sodium 122 mg Total Carbs 4.1 g Fiber 2 g Sugar 0.3 g Protein 7.7 g

Chocolate Chaffles

Servings: 2
Cooking Time: 10 Minutes
Ingredients:

- ¾ cup shredded mozzarella
- 1 large egg
- 2 Tbsp almond flour
- 2 Tbsp allulose
- ½ Tbsp melted butter
- 1½ Tbsp cocoa powder
- ½ tsp vanilla extract
- ½ tsp psyllium husk powder
- ¼ tsp baking powder

Directions:

1. Turn on waffle maker to heat and oil it with cooking spray.
2. Mix all ingredients in a small bowl.
3. Pour ¼ cup batter into a 4-inch waffle maker.
4. Cook for 2-3 minutes, or until crispy.
5. Transfer chaffle to a plate and set aside.
6. Repeat with remaining batter.

Nutrition Info: Carbs: 6 g ;Fat: 24 g ;Protein: 15 g ;Calories: 296

Strawberry Shortcake Chaffles

Servings: 1
Cooking Time: 25 Minutes
Ingredients:

- For the batter:
- 1 egg
- ¼ cup mozzarella cheese
- 1 Tbsp cream cheese
- ¼ tsp baking powder
- 2 strawberries, sliced
- 1 tsp strawberry extract
- For the glaze:
- 1 Tbsp cream cheese
- ¼ tsp strawberry extract
- 1 Tbsp monk fruit confectioners blend
- For the whipped cream:
- 1 cup heavy whipping cream
- 1 tsp vanilla
- 1 Tbsp monk fruit

Directions:

1. Turn on waffle maker to heat and oil it with cooking spray.
2. Beat egg in a small bowl.

3. Add remaining batter components.
4. Divide the mixture in half.
5. Cook one half of the batter in a waffle maker for 4 minutes, or until golden brown.
6. Repeat with remaining batter
7. Mix all glaze ingredients and spread over each warm chaffle.
8. Mix all whipped cream ingredients and whip until it starts to form peaks.
9. Top each waffle with whipped cream and strawberries.

Nutrition Info: Carbs: 5 g ;Fat: 14 g ;Protein: 12 g ;Calories: 218

Italian Cream Chaffle Sandwich-cake

Servings: 4
Cooking Time: 20 Minutes

Ingredients:

- 4 oz cream cheese, softened, at room temperature
- 4 eggs
- 1 Tbsp melted butter
- 1 tsp vanilla extract
- ½ tsp cinnamon
- 1 Tbsp monk fruit sweetener
- 4 Tbsp coconut flour
- 1 Tbsp almond flour
- 1½ teaspoons baking powder
- 1 Tbsp coconut, shredded and unsweetened
- 1 Tbsp walnuts, chopped
- For the Italian cream frosting:
- 2 oz cream cheese, softened, at room temperature
- 2 Tbsp butter room temp
- 2 Tbsp monk fruit sweetener
- ½ tsp vanilla

Directions:

1. Combine cream cheese, eggs, melted butter, vanilla, sweetener, flours, and baking powder in a blender.
2. Add walnuts and coconut to the mixture.
3. Blend to get a creamy mixture.
4. Turn on waffle maker to heat and oil it with cooking spray.
5. Add enough batter to fill waffle maker. Cook for 2-3 minutes, until chaffles are done.
6. Remove and let them cool.
7. Mix all frosting ingredients in another bowl. Stir until smooth and creamy.
8. Frost the chaffles once they have cooled.
9. Top with cream and more nuts.

Nutrition Info: Carbs: 31 g ;Fat: 2 g ;Protein: 5 g ;Calories: 168

Colby Jack Chaffles

Servings: 1
Cooking Time: 6 Minutes

Ingredients:

- 2 ounces colby jack cheese, sliced thinly in triangles
- 1 large organic egg, beaten

Directions:

1. Preheat a waffle iron and then grease it.
2. Arrange 1 thin layer of cheese slices in the bottom of preheated waffle iron.
3. Place the beaten egg on top of the cheese.
4. Now, arrange another layer of cheese slices on top to cover evenly.
5. Cook for about 5–6 minutes.
6. Serve warm.

Nutrition Info: Calories 292 Net Carbs 2.4 g Total Fat 23 g Saturated Fat 13.6 g Cholesterol 236 mg Sodium 431 mg Total Carbs 2.4 g Fiber 0 g Sugar 0.4 g Protein 18.3 g

Chaffle Glazed With Raspberry

Servings: 1
Cooking Time: 5 Minutes

Ingredients:

- Donut Chaffle Ingredients:
- 1 egg
- ¼ cup mozzarella cheese, shredded
- 2 tsp cream cheese, softened
- 1 tsp sweetener
- 1tsp almond flour
- ½ tsp baking powder
- 20 drops glazed donut flavoring
- Raspberry Jelly Filling:
- ¼ cup raspberries
- 1 tsp chia seeds
- 1 tsp confectioners sweetener
- Donut Glaze:
- 1 tsp powdered sweetener
- Heavy whipping cream
- Spray your waffle maker with cooking oil and add the batter mixture into the waffle maker.
- Cook for 3 minutes and set aside.
- Raspberry Jelly Filling:
- Mix all the
- Place in a pot and heat on medium.
- Gently mash the raspberries and set aside to cool.
- Donut Glaze:
- Stir together the
- Assembling:
- Lay your chaffles on a plate and add the fillings mixture between the layers.
- Drizzle the glaze on top and enjoy.

Directions:

1. Chaffles:
2. Preheat your waffle maker.

3. Mix all the chaffle

Nutrition Info: Calories Per Serving 188 Kcal; Fats: 23 g ; Carbs: 12 g ; Protein: 17 g

Carrot Chaffles

Servings: 6
Cooking Time: 18 Minutes

Ingredients:

- ¾ cup almond flour
- 1 tablespoon walnuts, chopped
- 2 tablespoons powdered Erythritol
- 1 teaspoon organic baking powder
- ½ teaspoon ground cinnamon
- ½ teaspoon pumpkin pie spice
- 1 organic egg, beaten
- 2 tablespoons heavy whipping cream
- 2 tablespoons butter, melted
- ½ cup carrot, peeled and shredded

Directions:

1. Preheat a mini waffle iron and then grease it.
2. In a bowl, place the flour, walnut, Erythritol, cinnamon, baking powder and spices and mix well.
3. Add the egg, heavy whipping cream and butter and mix until well combined.
4. Gently, fold in the carrot.
5. Add about 3 tablespoons of the mixture into preheated waffle iron and cook for about 2½-3 minutes or until golden brown.
6. Repeat with the remaining mixture.
7. Serve warm.

Nutrition Info: Per Serving Calories: 165Net Carb: 2.4gFat: 14.7gSaturated Fat: 4.4g Carbohydrates: 4.4gDietary Fiber: 2g Sugar: 1g Protein: 1.5g

Cream Cheese & Butter Chaffles

Servings: 4
Cooking Time: 16 Minutes

Ingredients:

- 2 tablespoons butter, melted and cooled
- 2 large organic eggs
- 2 ounces cream cheese, softened
- ¼ cup powdered Erythritol
- 1½ teaspoons organic vanilla extract
- Pinch of salt
- ¼ cup almond flour
- 2 tablespoons coconut flour
- 1 teaspoon organic baking powder

Directions:

1. Preheat a mini waffle iron and then grease it.

2. In a bowl, place the butter and eggs and beat until creamy.
3. Add the cream cheese, Erythritol, vanilla extract and salt and beat until well combined.
4. Add the flours and baking powder and beat until well combined.
5. Place ¼ of the mixture into preheated waffle iron and cook for about 4 minutes or until golden brown.
6. Repeat with the remaining mixture.
7. Serve warm.

Nutrition Info: Per Serving Calories: 202Net Carb: 2.8gFat: 17.3gSaturated Fat: 8g Carbohydrates: 5.1gDietary Fiber: 2.3g Sugar: 0.7g Protein: 4.8g

Yogurt Chaffles

Servings: 3
Cooking Time: 10 Minutes

Ingredients:

- ½ cup shredded mozzarella
- 1 egg
- 2 Tbsp ground almonds
- ½ tsp psyllium husk
- ¼ tsp baking powder
- 1 Tbsp yogurt

Directions:

1. Turn on waffle maker to heat and oil it with cooking spray.
2. Whisk eggs in a bowl.
3. Add in remaining ingredients except mozzarella and mix well.
4. Add mozzarella and mix once again. Let it sit for 5 minutes.
5. Add ⅓ cup batter into each waffle mold.
6. Close and cook for 4-5 minutes.
7. Repeat with remaining batter.

Nutrition Info: Carbs: 2 g ;Fat: 5 g ;Protein: 4 g ;Calories: 93

Chocolate Vanilla Chaffles

Servings: 2
Cooking Time: 5 Minutes

Ingredients:

- ½ cup shredded mozzarella cheese
- 1 egg
- 1 Tbsp granulated sweetener
- 1 tsp vanilla extract
- 1 Tbsp sugar-free chocolate chips
- 2 Tbsp almond meal/flour

Directions:

1. Turn on waffle maker to heat and oil it with cooking spray.
2. Mix all components in a bowl until combined.
3. Pour half of the batter into waffle maker.
4. Cook for 2-4 minutes, then remove and repeat with remaining batter.

5. Top with more chips and favorite toppings.

Nutrition Info: Carbs: 23 g ;Fat: 3 g ;Protein: 4 g ;Calories: 134

Strawberry Chaffles

Servings: 2

Cooking Time: 8 Minutes

Ingredients:

- 1 organic egg, beaten
- ¼ cup Mozzarella cheese, shredded
- 1 tablespoon cream cheese, softened
- ¼ teaspoon organic baking powder
- 1 teaspoon organic strawberry extract
- 2 fresh strawberries, hulled and sliced

Directions:

1. Preheat a mini waffle iron and then grease it.
2. In a bowl, place all ingredients except strawberry slices and beat until well combined.
3. Fold in the strawberry slices.
4. Place half of the mixture into preheated waffle iron and cook for about 4 minutes or until golden brown.
5. Repeat with the remaining mixture.
6. Serve warm.

Nutrition Info: Per Serving Calories: 69Net Carb: 1.6gFat: 4.6gSaturated Fat: 2.2g Carbohydrates: 1.9gDietary Fiber: 0.3g Sugar: 1g Protein: 4.2g

Blueberry Cream Cheese Chaffles

Servings: 2

Cooking Time: 8 Minutes

Ingredients:

- 1 organic egg, beaten
- 1 tablespoon cream cheese, softened
- 3 tablespoons almond flour
- ¼ teaspoon organic baking powder
- 1 teaspoon organic blueberry extract
- 5-6 fresh blueberries

Directions:

1. Preheat a mini waffle iron and then grease it.
2. In a bowl, place all the ingredients except blueberries and beat until well combined.
3. Fold in the blueberries.
4. Divide the mixture into 5 portions.
5. Place 1 portion of the mixture into preheated waffle iron and cook for about 3-4 minutes or until golden brown.
6. Repeat with the remaining mixture.
7. Serve warm.

Nutrition Info: Per Serving Calories: 120Net Carb: 1.8gFat: 9.6gSaturated Fat: 2.2g Carbohydrates: 3.1gDietary Fiber: 1.3g Sugar: 1g Protein: 3.2g

Almond Flour Chaffles

Servings: 2
Cooking Time: 20 Minutes
Ingredients:

- 1 large egg
- 1 Tbsp blanched almond flour
- ¼ tsp baking powder
- ½ cup shredded mozzarella cheese

Directions:

1. Whisk egg, almond flour, and baking powder together.
2. Stir in mozzarella and set batter aside.
3. Turn on waffle maker to heat and oil it with cooking spray.
4. Pour half of the batter onto waffle maker and spread it evenly with a spoon.
5. Cook for 3 minutes, or until it reaches desired doneness.
6. Transfer to a plate and repeat with remaining batter.
7. Let chaffles cool for 2-3 minutes to crisp up.

Nutrition Info: Carbs: 2 g ;Fat: 13 g ;Protein: 10 g ;Calories: 131

Chocolate Chips & Whipping Cream Chaffles

Servings: 2
Cooking Time: 8 Minutes
Ingredients:

- 1 organic egg
- 1 tablespoon heavy whipping cream
- ½ teaspoon coconut flour
- 1¾ teaspoons monkfruit sweetener
- ¼ teaspoon organic baking powder
- Pinch of salt
- 1 tablespoon 70% dark chocolate chips

Directions:

1. Preheat a mini waffle iron and then grease it.
2. In a bowl, place all ingredients except for chocolate chips and beat until well combined.
3. Fold in the blackberries.
4. Place half of the mixture into preheated waffle iron and top with half of the chocolate chips.
5. Cook for about 3-4 minutes or until golden brown.
6. Repeat with the remaining mixture and chocolate chips.
7. Serve warm.

Nutrition Info: Per Serving Calories: 110Net Carb: 1.8gFat: 9gSaturated Fat: 5g Carbohydrates: 3.1gDietary Fiber: 1.3g Sugar: 0.2g Protein: 4g

Banana Nut Chaffle

Servings: 1
Cooking Time: 10 Minutes

Ingredients:

- 1 egg
- 1 Tbsp cream cheese, softened and room temp
- 1 Tbsp sugar-free cheesecake pudding
- ½ cup mozzarella cheese
- 1 Tbsp monk fruit confectioners sweetener
- ¼ tsp vanilla extract
- ¼ tsp banana extract
- toppings of choice

Directions:

1. Turn on waffle maker to heat and oil it with cooking spray.
2. Beat egg in a small bowl.
3. Add remaining ingredients and mix until well incorporated.
4. Add one half of the batter to waffle maker and cook for 4 minutes, until golden brown.
5. Remove chaffle and add the other half of the batter.
6. Top with your optional toppings and serve warm!

Nutrition Info: Carbs: 2 g ;Fat: 7 g ;Protein: 8 g ;Calories: 119

Almond Butter Chaffles

Servings: 2
Cooking Time: 10 Minutes

Ingredients:

- 1 large organic egg, beaten
- 1/3 cup Mozzarella cheese, shredded
- 1 tablespoon Erythritol
- 2 tablespoons almond butter
- 1 teaspoon organic vanilla extract

Directions:

1. Preheat a mini waffle iron and then grease it.
2. In a medium bowl, place all ingredients and with a fork, mix until well combined.
3. Place half of the mixture into preheated waffle iron and cook for about 3-5 minutes or until golden brown.
4. Repeat with the remaining mixture.
5. Serve warm.

Nutrition Info: Per Serving Calories: 153Net Carb: 2gFat: 12.3gSaturated Fat: 2g Carbohydrates: 3.6gDietary Fiber: 1.6g Sugar: 1.2g Protein: 7.9g

Chocolaty Chips Pumpkin Chaffles

Servings: 3
Cooking Time: 12 Minutes

Ingredients:

- 1 organic egg
- 4 teaspoons homemade pumpkin puree
- ½ cup Mozzarella cheese, shredded
- 1 tablespoon almond flour

- 2 tablespoons granulated Erythritol
- ¼ teaspoon pumpkin pie spice
- 4 teaspoons 70% dark chocolate chips

Directions:

1. In a bowl, place the egg and pumpkin puree and mix well.
2. Add the remaining ingredients except for chocolate chips and mix until well combined.
3. Gently, fold in the chocolate chips and lemon zest.
4. Place 1/3 of the mixture into preheated waffle iron and cook for about 4 minutes or until golden brown.
5. Repeat with the remaining mixture.
6. Serve warm.

Nutrition Info: Per Serving Calories: 97Net Carb: 1.9gFat: 7.1gSaturated Fat: 3.3g Carbohydrates: 1.4gDietary Fiber: 2.6g Sugar: 0.4g Protein: 4.2g

CHAFFLE CAKE & SANDWICH RECIPES

Strawberry Cream Sandwich Chaffles

Servings: 2
Cooking Time: 6 Minutes

Ingredients:

- Chaffles
- 1 large organic egg, beaten
- ½ cup mozzarella cheese, shredded finely
- Filling
- 4 teaspoons heavy cream
- 2 tablespoons powdered erythritol
- 1 teaspoon fresh lemon juice
- Pinch of fresh lemon zest, grated
- 2 fresh strawberries, hulled and sliced

Directions:

1. Preheat a mini waffle iron and then grease it.
2. For chaffles: in a small bowl, add the egg and mozzarella cheese and stir to combine.
3. Place half of the mixture into preheated waffle iron and cook for about 2–3 minutes.
4. Repeat with the remaining mixture.
5. Meanwhile, for filling: in a bowl, Place all the ingredients except the strawberry slices and with a hand mixer, beat until well combined.
6. Serve each chaffle with cream mixture and strawberry slices.

Nutrition Info: Calories 95 Net Carbs 1.4 g Total Fat 7.5 g Saturated Fat 3.9 g Cholesterol 110 mg Sodium 82 mg Total Carbs 1.7 g Fiber 0.3 g Sugar 0.9 g Protein 5.5 g

Egg & Bacon Sandwich Chaffles

Servings: 4
Cooking Time: 20 Minutes

Ingredients:

- Chaffles
- 2 large organic eggs, beaten
- 4 tablespoons almond flour
- 1 teaspoon organic baking powder
- 1 cup mozzarella cheese, shredded
- Filling
- 4 organic fried eggs
- 4 cooked bacon slices

Directions:

1. Preheat a mini waffle iron and then grease it.
2. In a medium bowl, put all ingredients and with a fork, mix until well combined.Place half of the mixture into preheated waffle iron and cook for about 3–5 minutes.
3. Repeat with the remaining mixture.
4. Repeat with the remaining mixture.
5. Serve each chaffle with filling ingredients.

Nutrition Info: Calories 197 Net Carb: g Total Fat 14.5 g Saturated Fat 4.1 g Cholesterol 267 mg Sodium 224 g Total Carbs 2.7 g Fiber 0.8 g Sugar 0.8 g Protein 12.9 g

Blueberry Peanut Butter Sandwich Chaffles

Servings: 2
Cooking Time: 10 Minutes

Ingredients:

- 1 organic egg, beaten
- ½ cup cheddar cheese, shredded
- Filling
- 2 tablespoons erythritol
- 1 tablespoon butter, softened
- 1 tablespoon natural peanut butter
- 2 tablespoons cream cheese, softened
- ¼ teaspoon organic vanilla extract
- 2 teaspoons fresh blueberries

Directions:

1. Preheat a mini waffle iron and then grease it.
2. For chaffles: in a small bowl, add the egg and Cheddar cheese and stir to combine.
3. Place half of the mixture into preheated waffle iron and cook for about 3–5 minutes.
4. Repeat with the remaining mixture.
5. Meanwhile, for filling: In a medium bowl, put all ingredients and mix until well combined.
6. Serve each chaffle with peanut butter mixture.

Nutrition Info: Calories 143 Net Carbs 3.3 g Total Fat 10.1 g Saturated Fat 4.5 g Cholesterol 100 mg Sodium 148 mg Total Carbs 4.1 g Fiber 0.8 g Sugar 1.2 g Protein 7.6 g

Strawberry Shortcake Chaffle

Servings: 3
Cooking Time: 12 Minutes

Ingredients:

- Strawberry topping Ingredients:
- 3 fresh strawberries
- 1/2 tablespoon granulated swerve
- Sweet Chaffle Ingredients:
- 1 tablespoon almond flour
- 1/2 cup mozzarella cheese
- 1 egg
- 1 tablespoon granulated swerve
- 1/4 teaspoon vanilla extract
- Keto Whipped Cream

Directions:

1. Heat up your waffle maker. If you are using a mini waffle maker, this recipe will make 2 chaffles; if using a large waffle maker, this recipe will make 1 large sweet chaffle.
2. Rinse and chop up your fresh strawberries. Place the strawberries in a small bowl and add 1/2 tablespoon granulated swerve. Mix the strawberries with the swerve and set aside.

3. In a bowl mix the almond flour, egg, mozzarella cheese, granulated swerve and vanilla extract.
4. Pour 1/3 of the batter into your mini waffle maker and cook for 3-4 minutes. Then cook another 1/3 of the batter and the rest of the batter to make 3 keto chaffles.
5. While your second chaffle is cooking, make your keto whipped cream if you do not have any on hand.
6. Assemble your Strawberry Shortcake Chaffle by placing whipped cream and strawberries on top of your sweet chaffle. Then drizzle the juice that will also be in the bowl with the strawberries on top.

Nutrition Info: (Per Serving):Calories: 112kcal;Carbohydrates:2g;Protein: 7g;Fat: 8g;Saturated Fat:3g;Cholesterol:69mg;Sodium:138mg;Potassium: 53mg;Fiber: 1g;Sugar: 1g;Vitamin A: 205IU;Vitamin C: 7mg;Calcium: 107mg;Iron: 1mg

Salmon & Cheese Sandwich Chaffles

Servings: 4
Cooking Time: 24 Minutes

Ingredients:

- Chaffles
- 2 organic eggs
- ½ ounce butter, melted
- 1 cup mozzarella cheese, shredded
- 2 tablespoons almond flour
- Pinch of salt
- Filling
- ½ cup smoked salmon
- 1/3 cup avocado, peeled, pitted, and sliced
- 2 tablespoons feta cheese, crumbled

Directions:

1. Preheat a mini waffle iron and then grease it.
2. For chaffles: In a medium bowl, put all ingredients and with a fork, mix until well combined.Place ¼ of the mixture into preheated waffle iron and cook for about 5–6 minutes.
3. Repeat with the remaining mixture.
4. Serve each chaffle with filling ingredients.

Nutrition Info: Calories 169 Net Carbs 1.2 g Total Fat 13.5 g Saturated Fat 5 g Cholesterol 101 mg Sodium 319 mg Total Carbs 2.8 g Fiber 1.6 g Sugar 0.6 g Protein 8.9 g

Strawberry Cream Cheese Sandwich Chaffles

Servings: 2
Cooking Time: 10 Minutes

Ingredients:

- Chaffles
- 1 organic egg, beaten
- 1 teaspoon organic vanilla extract
- 1 tablespoon almond flour
- 1 teaspoon organic baking powder

- Pinch of ground cinnamon
- 1 cup mozzarella cheese, shredded
- Filling
- 2 tablespoons cream cheese, softened
- 2 tablespoons erythritol
- ¼ teaspoon organic vanilla extract
- 2 fresh strawberries, hulled and chopped

Directions:

1. Preheat a mini waffle iron and then grease it.
2. For chaffles: in a bowl, add the egg and vanilla extract and mix well.
3. Add the flour, baking powder, and cinnamon, and mix until well combined.
4. Add the mozzarella cheese and stir to combine.
5. Place half of the mixture into preheated waffle iron and cook for about 4–5 minutes.
6. Repeat with the remaining mixture.
7. Meanwhile, for filling: in a bowl, Place all the ingredients except the strawberry pieces and with a hand mixer, beat until well combined.
8. Serve each chaffle with cream cheese mixture and strawberry pieces.

Nutrition Info: Calories 143 Net Carb: g Total Fat 10.1 g Saturated Fat 4.5 g Cholesterol 100 mg Sodium 148 mg Total Carbs 4.1 g Fiber 0.8 g Sugar 1.2 g Protein 7.6 g

Chocolate Sandwich Chaffles

Servings: 2
Cooking Time: 10 Minutes

Ingredients:

- Chaffles
- 1 organic egg, beaten
- 1 ounce cream cheese, softened
- 2 tablespoons almond flour
- 1 tablespoon cacao powder
- 2 teaspoons erythritol
- 1 teaspoon organic vanilla extract
- Filling
- 2 tablespoons cream cheese, softened
- 2 tablespoons erythritol
- ½ tablespoon cacao powder
- ¼ teaspoon organic vanilla extract

Directions:

1. Preheat a mini waffle iron and then grease it.
2. For chaffles: In a medium bowl, put all ingredients and with a fork, mix until well combined.Place half of the mixture into preheated waffle iron and cook for about 3–5 minutes.
3. Repeat with the remaining mixture.
4. Meanwhile, for filling: In a medium bowl, put all ingredients and with a hand mixer, beat until well combined.
5. Serve each chaffle with chocolate mixture.

Nutrition Info: Calories 192 Net Carb: g Total Fat 16.6 g Saturated Fat 7.6 g Cholesterol 113 mg Sodium 115 mg Total Carbs 4.4 g Fiber 1.9 g Sugar 0.8 g Protein 5.7 g

Berry Sauce Sandwich Chaffles

Servings: 2
Cooking Time: 8 Minutes

Ingredients:

- Filling
- 3 ounces frozen mixed berries, thawed with the juice
- 1 tablespoon erythritol
- 1 tablespoon water
- ¼ tablespoon fresh lemon juice
- 2 teaspoons cream
- Chaffles
- 1 large organic egg, beaten
- ½ cup cheddar cheese, shredded
- 2 tablespoons almond flour

Directions:

1. For berry sauce: in a pan, add the berries, erythritol, water and lemon juice over medium heat and cook for about 8-10 minutes, pressing with the spoon occasionally.
2. Remove the pan of sauce from heat and set aside to cool before serving.
3. Preheat a mini waffle iron and then grease it.
4. In a bowl, add the egg, cheddar cheese and almond flour and beat until well combined.Place half of the mixture into preheated waffle iron and cook for about 3-5 minutes.
5. Repeat with the remaining mixture.
6. Serve each chaffle with cream and berry sauce.

Nutrition Info: Calories 222 Net Carbs 4.7 g Total Fat 16 g Saturated Fat 7.2 g Cholesterol 123 mg Sodium 212 mg Total Carbs 7 g Fiber 2.3 g Sugar 3.8 g Protein 10.5 g

Pork Sandwich Chaffles

Servings: 4
Cooking Time: 16 Minutes

Ingredients:

- Chaffles
- 2 large organic eggs
- ¼ cup superfine blanched almond flour
- ¾ teaspoon organic baking powder
- ½ teaspoon garlic powder
- 1 cup cheddar cheese, shredded
- Filling
- 12 ounces cooked pork, cut into slices
- 1 tomato, sliced
- 4 lettuce leaves

Directions:

1. Preheat a mini waffle iron and then grease it.
2. For chaffles: in a bowl, add the eggs, almond flour, baking powder, and garlic powder, and beat until well combined.

3. Add the cheese and stir to combine.
4. Place ¼ of the mixture into preheated waffle iron and cook for about 3–4 minutes.
5. Repeat with the remaining mixture.
6. Serve each chaffle with filling ingredients.

Nutrition Info: Calories 319 Net Carbs 2.5 g Total Fat 18.2 g Saturated Fat 8 g Cholesterol 185 mg Sodium 263 mg Total Carbs 3.5 g Fiber 1 g Sugar 0.9 g Protein 34.2 g

Tomato Sandwich Chaffles

Servings: 2
Cooking Time: 6 Minutes

Ingredients:

- Chaffles
- 1 large organic egg, beaten
- ½ cup colby jack cheese, shredded finely
- 1/8 teaspoon organic vanilla extract
- Filling
- 1 small tomato, sliced
- 2 teaspoons fresh basil leaves

Directions:

1. Preheat a mini waffle iron and then grease it.
2. For chaffles: in a small bowl, place all the ingredients and stir to combine.
3. Place half of the mixture into preheated waffle iron and cook for about 3 minutes.
4. Repeat with the remaining mixture.
5. Serve each chaffle with tomato slices and basil leaves.

Nutrition Info: Calories 155 Net Carbs 2.4 g Total Fat 11.6 g Saturated Fat 6.8 g Cholesterol 118 mg Sodium 217 mg Total Carbs 3 g Fiber 0.6 g Sugar 1.4 g Protein 9.6 g

Ham Sandwich Chaffles

Servings: 2
Cooking Time: 8 Minutes

Ingredients:

- 1 organic egg, beaten
- ½ cup Monterrey Jack cheese, shredded
- 1 teaspoon coconut flour
- Pinch of garlic powder
- Filling
- 2 sugar-free ham slices
- 1 small tomato, sliced
- 2 lettuce leaves

Directions:

1. Preheat a mini waffle iron and then grease it.
2. For chaffles: In a medium bowl, put all ingredients and with a fork, mix until well combined.Place half of the mixture into preheated waffle iron and cook for about 3–4 minutes.
3. Repeat with the remaining mixture.
4. Serve each chaffle with filling ingredients.

Nutrition Info: Calories 156 Net Carbs 3.7 g Total Fat 8.7 g Saturated Fat 3.4 g Cholesterol 114 mg Sodium 794 mg Total Carbs 5.5 g Fiber 1.8 g Sugar 1.5 g Protein 13.9 g

Chocolate Chaffle Cake

Servings: 2
Cooking Time: 8 Minutes

Ingredients:

- Chocolate Chaffle Cake Ingredients:
- 2 tablespoons cocoa powder
- 2 tablespoons Swerve granulated sweetener
- 1 egg
- 1 tablespoon heavy whipping cream
- 1 tablespoon almond flour
- 1/4 tsp baking powder
- 1/2 tsp vanilla extract
- Cream Cheese Frosting:
- 2 tablespoons cream cheese
- 2 teaspoons swerve confectioners
- 1/8 tsp vanilla extract
- 1 tsp heavy cream

Directions:

1. How to Make Chocolate Chaffle Cake:
2. In a small bowl, whisk together cocoa powder, swerve, almond flour, and baking powder.
3. Add in the vanilla extract and heavy whipping cream and mix well.
4. Add in the egg and mix well. Be sure to scrape the sides of the bowl to get all of the ingredients mixed well.
5. Let sit for 3-4 minutes while the mini waffle maker heats up.
6. Add half of the waffle mixture to the waffle maker and cook for 4 minutes. Then cook the second waffle. While the second chocolate keto waffle is cooking, make your frosting.
7. How to Make Cream Cheese Frosting:
8. In a small microwave-safe bowl add 2 tablespoons cream cheese. Microwave the cream cheese for 8 seconds to soften the cream cheese.
9. Add in heavy whipping cream and vanilla extract and use a small hand mixer to mix well.
10. Then add in the confectioners swerve and use the hand mixer to incorporate and fluffy the frosting.
11. Assembling Keto Chocolate Chaffle cake:
12. Place one chocolate chaffle on a plate, top with a layer of frosting. You can spread it with a knife or use a pastry bag and pipe the frosting.
13. Put the second chocolate chaffle on top of the frosting layer and then spread or pipe the rest of the frosting on top.

Nutrition Info: (Per Serving):Calories: 151kcal ;Carbohydrates:5g ;Protein: 6g;Fat: 13g ;Saturated Fat:6g ;Cholesterol:111mg ;Sodium:83mg ;Potassium: 190mg ;Fiber: 2g ;Sugar: 1g ;Vitamin A: 461IU ;Calcium: 67mg ;Iron: 1mg

Salmon & Cream Sandwich Chaffles

Servings: 2
Cooking Time: 8 Minutes

Ingredients:

- Chaffles
- 1 organic egg, beaten
- ½ cup cheddar cheese, shredded
- 1 tablespoon almond flour
- 1 tablespoon fresh rosemary, chopped
- Filling
- ¼ cup smoked salmon
- 1 teaspoon fresh dill, chopped
- 2 tablespoons cream

Directions:

1. Preheat a mini waffle iron and then grease it.
2. For chaffles: In a medium bowl, put all ingredients and with a fork, mix until well combined.Place half of the mixture into preheated waffle iron and cook for about 3–4 minutes.
3. Repeat with the remaining mixture.
4. Serve each chaffle with filling ingredients.

Nutrition Info: Calories 202 Net Carbs 1.7 g Total Fat 15.1 g Saturated Fat 7.5 g Cholesterol 118 mg Sodium 345 mg Total Carbs 2.9 g Fiber 1.2 g Sugar 0.7 g Protein 13.2 g

Chicken Sandwich Chaffles

Servings: 2
Cooking Time: 8 Minutes

Ingredients:

- Chaffles
- 1 large organic egg, beaten
- ½ cup cheddar cheese, shredded
- Pinch of salt and ground black pepper
- Filling
- 1 (6-ounce) cooked chicken breast, halved
- 2 lettuce leaves
- ¼ of small onion, sliced
- 1 small tomato, sliced

Directions:

1. Preheat a mini waffle iron and then grease it.
2. For chaffles: In a medium bowl, put all ingredients and with a fork, mix until well combined.Place half of the mixture into preheated waffle iron and cook for about 3–4 minutes.
3. Repeat with the remaining mixture.
4. Serve each chaffle with filling ingredients.

Nutrition Info: Calories 259 Net Carbs 2.5 g Total Fat 14.1 g Saturated Fat 6.8 g Cholesterol 177 mg Sodium 334 mg Total Carbs 3.3 g Fiber 0.8 g Sugar 2 g Protein 28.7 g

Tuna Sandwich Chaffles

Servings: 2
Cooking Time: 8 Minutes

Ingredients:

- Chaffles
- 1 organic egg, beaten
- ½ cup cheddar cheese, shredded
- 1 tablespoon almond flour
- Pinch of salt
- Filling
- ¼ cup water-packed tuna, flaked
- 2 lettuce leaves

Directions:

1. Preheat a mini waffle iron and then grease it.
2. For chaffles: In a medium bowl, put all ingredients and with a fork, mix until well combined.Place half of the mixture into preheated waffle iron and cook for about 3–4 minutes.
3. Repeat with the remaining mixture.
4. Serve each chaffle with filling ingredients.

Nutrition Info: Calories 186 Net Carbs 0.9 g Total Fat 13.6 g Saturated Fat 6.8 g Cholesterol 120 mg Sodium 342 mg Total Carbs 1.3 g Fiber 0.4 g Sugar 0.5 g Protein 13.6 g

VEGETARIAN CHAFFLE RECIPES

Fruity Vegan Chaffles

Servings: 2
Cooking Time: 5minutes
Ingredients:

- 1 tbsp. chia seeds
- 2 tbsps. warm water
- ¼ cup low carb vegan cheese
- 2 tbsps. strawberry puree
- 2 tbsps. Greek yogurt
- pinch of salt

Directions:

1. Preheat waffle maker to medium-high heat.
2. In a small bowl, mix together chia seeds and water and let it stand for few minutes to be thickened.
3. Mix the rest of the ingredients in chia seed egg and mix well.
4. Spray waffle machine with cooking spray.
5. Pour vegan waffle batter into the center of the waffle iron.
6. Close the waffle maker and cook chaffles for about 3-5 minutes.
7. Once cooked, remove from the maker and serve with berries on top.

Nutrition Info: Per Serving: Protein: 32% 42 kcal Fat: 63% 82 kcal Carbohydrates: 5% 6 kcal

Broccoli Chaffle

Servings: 4
Cooking Time: 15 Minutes
Ingredients:

- Batter
- 4 eggs
- 2 cups grated mozzarella cheese
- 1 cup steamed broccoli, chopped
- Salt and pepper to taste
- 1 clove garlic, minced
- 1 teaspoon chili flakes
- 2 tablespoons almond flour
- 2 teaspoons baking powder
- Other
- 2 tablespoons cooking spray to brush the waffle maker
- ¼ cup mascarpone cheese for serving

Directions:

1. Preheat the waffle maker.
2. Add the eggs, grated mozzarella, chopped broccoli, salt and pepper, minced garlic, chili flakes, almond flour and baking powder to a bowl.
3. Mix with a fork.
4. Brush the heated waffle maker with cooking spray and add a few tablespoons of the batter.
5. Close the lid and cook for about 5–7 minutes depending on your waffle maker.

6. Serve each chaffle with mascarpone cheese.

Nutrition Info: Per Serving Calories 229, fat 17.5 g, carbs 6 g, sugar 1.1 g, Protein 13.1 g, sodium 194 mg

Vegan Chocolate Chaffles

Servings: 2
Cooking Time: 5minutes

Ingredients:

- 1/2 cupcoconut flour
- 3 tbsps. cocoa powder
- 2 tbsps. whole psyllium husk
- 1/2 teaspoon baking powder
- pinch of salt
- 1/2 cup vegan cheese, softened
- 1/4 cup coconut milk

Directions:

1. Prepare your waffle iron according to the manufacturer's instructions.
2. Mix together coconut flour, cocoa powder, baking powder, salt and husk in a bowl and set aside.
3. Add melted cheese and milk and mix well. Let it stand for a few minutes before cooking.
4. Pour batter in waffle machine and cook for about 3-4 minutes.
5. Once chaffles are cooked, carefully remove them from the waffle machine.
6. Serve with vegan icecream and enjoy!

Nutrition Info: Per Serving: Protein: 32% 42 kcal Fat: 63% 82 kcal Carbohydrates: 5% 6 kcal

Avocado Croque Madam Chaffle

Servings: 4
Cooking Time: 15 Minutes

Ingredients:

- Batter
- 4 eggs
- 2 cups grated mozzarella cheese
- 1 avocado, mashed
- Salt and pepper to taste
- 6 tablespoons almond flour
- 2 teaspoons baking powder
- 1 teaspoon dried dill
- Other
- 2 tablespoons cooking spray to brush the waffle maker
- 4 fried eggs
- 2 tablespoons freshly chopped basil

Directions:

1. Preheat the waffle maker.
2. Add the eggs, grated mozzarella, avocado, salt and pepper, almond flour, baking powder and dried dill to a bowl.

3. Mix with a fork.
4. Brush the heated waffle maker with cooking spray and add a few tablespoons of the batter.
5. Close the lid and cook for about 5–7 minutes depending on your waffle maker.
6. Serve each chaffle with a fried egg and freshly chopped basil on top.

Nutrition Info: Per Serving Calories 393, fat 32.1 g, carbs 9.2 g, sugar 1.3 g, Protein 18.8 g, sodium 245 mg

Spinach And Artichoke Chaffle

Servings: 4
Cooking Time: 15 Minutes
Ingredients:

- Batter
- 4 eggs
- 2 cups grated provolone cheese
- 1 cup cooked and diced spinach
- ½ cup diced artichoke hearts
- Salt and pepper to taste
- 2 tablespoons coconut flour
- 2 teaspoons baking powder
- Other
- 2 tablespoons cooking spray to brush the waffle maker
- ¼ cup of cream cheese for serving

Directions:

1. Preheat the waffle maker.
2. Add the eggs, grated provolone cheese, diced spinach, artichoke hearts, salt and pepper, coconut flour and baking powder to a bowl.
3. Mix with a fork.
4. Brush the heated waffle maker with cooking spray and add a few tablespoons of the batter.
5. Close the lid and cook for about 5–7 minutes depending on your waffle maker.
6. Serve each chaffle with cream cheese.

Nutrition Info: Per Serving Calories 427, fat 32.8 g, carbs 9.5 g, sugar 1.1 g, Protein 25.7 g, sodium 722 mg

Garlic Mayo Vegan Chaffles

Servings: 2
Cooking Time: 5minutes
Ingredients:

- 1 tbsp. chia seeds
- 2 ½ tbsps. water
- ¼ cup low carb vegan cheese
- 2 tbsps. coconut flour
- 1 cup low carb vegan cream cheese, softened
- 1 tsp. garlic powder
- pinch of salt
- 2 tbsps. vegan garlic mayo for topping

Directions:

1. Preheat your square waffle maker.
2. In a small bowl, mix chia seeds and water, let it stand for 5 minutes.
3. Add all ingredients to the chia seeds mixture and mix well.
4. Pour vegan chaffle batter in a greased waffle maker
5. Close the waffle maker and cook for about 3-5 minutes.
6. Once chaffles are cooked, remove from the maker.
7. Top with garlic mayo and pepper.
8. Enjoy!

Nutrition Info: Per Serving: Protein: 32% 42 kcal Fat: 63% 82 kcal Carbohydrates: 5% 6 kcal

Asparagus Chaffle

Servings: 4
Cooking Time: 15 Minutes
Ingredients:

- Batter
- 4 eggs
- 1½ cups grated mozzarella cheese
- ½ cup grated parmesan cheese
- 1 cup boiled asparagus, chopped
- Salt and pepper to taste
- ¼ cup almond flour
- 2 teaspoons baking powder
- Other
- 2 tablespoons cooking spray to brush the waffle maker
- ¼ cup Greek yogurt for serving
- ¼ cup chopped almonds for serving

Directions:

1. Preheat the waffle maker.
2. Add the eggs, grated mozzarella, grated parmesan, asparagus, salt and pepper, almond flour and baking powder to a bowl.
3. Mix with a fork.
4. Brush the heated waffle maker with cooking spray and add a few tablespoons of the batter.
5. Close the lid and cook for about 5–7 minutes depending on your waffle maker.
6. Serve each chaffle with Greek yogurt and chopped almonds.

Nutrition Info: Per Serving Calories 316, fat 24.9 g, carbs 7.3 g, sugar 1.2 g, Protein 18.2 g, sodium 261 mg

Mushroom And Almond Chaffle

Servings: 4
Cooking Time: 15 Minutes
Ingredients:

- Batter
- 4 eggs
- 2 cups grated mozzarella cheese

- 1 cup finely chopped zucchini
- 3 tablespoons chopped almonds
- 2 teaspoons baking powder
- Salt and pepper to taste
- 1 teaspoon dried basil
- 1 teaspoon chili flakes
- Other
- 2 tablespoons cooking spray to brush the waffle maker

Directions:

1. Preheat the waffle maker.
2. Add the eggs, grated mozzarella, mushrooms, almonds, baking powder, salt and pepper, dried basil and chili flakes to a bowl.
3. Mix with a fork.
4. Brush the heated waffle maker with cooking spray and add a few tablespoons of the batter.
5. Close the lid and cook for about 5–7 minutes depending on your waffle maker.
6. Serve and enjoy.

Nutrition Info: Per Serving Calories 196, fat 16 g, carbs 4 g, sugar 1 g, Protein 10.8 g, sodium 152 mg

Celery And Cottage Cheese Chaffle

Servings: 4
Cooking Time: 15 Minutes
Ingredients:

- Batter
- 4 eggs
- 2 cups grated cheddar cheese
- 1 cup fresh celery, chopped
- Salt and pepper to taste
- 2 tablespoons chopped almonds
- 2 teaspoons baking powder
- Other
- 2 tablespoons cooking spray to brush the waffle maker
- ¼ cup cottage cheese for serving

Directions:

1. Preheat the waffle maker.
2. Add the eggs, grated mozzarella cheese, chopped celery, salt and pepper, chopped almonds and baking powder to a bowl.
3. Mix with a fork.
4. Brush the heated waffle maker with cooking spray and add a few tablespoons of the batter.
5. Close the lid and cook for about 5–7 minutes depending on your waffle maker.
6. Serve each chaffle with cottage cheese on top.

Nutrition Info: Per Serving Calories 385, fat 31.6 g, carbs 4 g, sugar 1.5 g, Protein 22.2 g, sodium 492 mg

Almonds And Flaxseeds Chaffles

Servings: 2
Cooking Time: 5minutes

Ingredients:

- 1/4 cup coconut flour
- 1 tsp. stevia
- 1 tbsp. ground flaxseed
- 1/4 tsp baking powder
- 1/2 cup almond milk
- 1/4 tsp vanilla extract
- 1/ cup low carb vegan cheese

Directions:

1. Mix together flaxseed in warm water and set aside.
2. Add in the remaining ingredients.
3. Switch on waffle iron and grease with cooking spray.
4. Pour the batter in the waffle machine and close the lid.
5. Cook the chaffles for about 3-4 minutes.
6. Once cooked, remove from the waffle machine.
7. Serve with berries and enjoy!

Nutrition Info: Per Serving: Protein: 32% 42 kcal Fat: 63% 82 kcal Carbohydrates: 5% 6 kcal

Vegan Chaffles With Flaxseed

Servings: 2
Cooking Time: 5minutes

Ingredients:

- 1 tbsp. flaxseed meal
- 2 tbsps. warm water
- ¼ cup low carb vegan cheese
- ¼ cup chopped minutest
- pinch of salt
- 2 oz. blueberries chunks

Directions:

1. Preheat waffle maker to medium-high heat and grease with cooking spray.
2. Mix together flaxseed meal and warm water and set aside to be thickened.
3. After 5 minutes' mix together all ingredients in flax egg.
4. Pour vegan waffle batter into the center of the waffle iron.
5. Close the waffle maker and let cook for 3-5 minutes
6. Once cooked, remove the vegan chaffle from the waffle maker and serve.

Nutrition Info: Per Serving: Protein: 32% 42 kcal Fat: 63% 82 kcal Carbohydrates: 5% 6 kcal

SAVORY CHAFFLES RECIPES

Bacon & Jalapeño Chaffles

Servings: 5
Cooking Time: 15 Minutes
Ingredients:

- 3 tablespoons coconut flour
- 1 teaspoon organic baking powder
- ¼ teaspoon salt
- ½ cup cream cheese, softened
- 3 large organic eggs
- 1 cup sharp Cheddar cheese, shredded
- 1 jalapeño pepper, seeded and chopped
- 3 cooked bacon slices, crumbled

Directions:

1. Preheat a mini waffle iron and then grease it.
2. In a small bowl, place the flour, baking powder and salt and mix well.
3. In a large bowl, place the cream cheese and beat until light and fluffy.
4. Add the eggs and Cheddar cheese and beat until well combined.
5. Add the flour mixture and beat until combined.
6. Fold in the jalapeño pepper.
7. Divide the mixture into 5 portions.
8. Place 1 portion of the mixture into preheated waffle iron and cook for about 5 minutes or until golden brown.
9. Repeat with the remaining mixture.
10. Serve warm with the topping of bacon pieces.

Nutrition Info: Per Serving Calories: 249Net Carb: 2.9gFat: 20.3gSaturated Fat: 11.5g Carbohydrates: 4.8gDietary Fiber: 1.9g Sugar: 0.5g Protein: 12.7g

Herb Chaffles

Servings: 4
Cooking Time: 12 Minutes
Ingredients:

- 4 tablespoons almond flour
- 1 tablespoon coconut flour
- 1 teaspoon mixed dried herbs
- ½ teaspoon organic baking powder
- ¼ teaspoon garlic powder
- ¼ teaspoon onion powder
- Salt and ground black pepper, to taste
- ¼ cup cream cheese, softened
- 3 large organic eggs
- ½ cup cheddar cheese, grated
- 1/3 cup Parmesan cheese, grated

Directions:

1. Preheat a waffle iron and then grease it.

2. In a bowl, mix together the flours, dried herbs, baking powder, and seasoning, and mix well.
3. In a separate bowl, put cream cheese and eggs and beat until well combined.
4. Add the flour mixture, cheddar, and Parmesan cheese, and mix until well combined.
5. Place the desired amount of the mixture into preheated waffle iron and cook for about 2–3 minutes.
6. Repeat with the remaining mixture.
7. Serve warm.

Nutrition Info: Calories 240 Net Carb: g Total Fat 19 g Saturated Fat 8.5 g Cholesterol 176 mg Sodium 280 mg Total Carbs 4 g Fiber 1.6 g Sugar 0.7 g Protein 12.3 g

Rosemary Chaffles

Servings: 2
Cooking Time: 8 Minutes

Ingredients:

- 1 organic egg, beaten
- ½ cup Cheddar cheese, shredded
- 1 tablespoon almond flour
- 1 tablespoon fresh rosemary, chopped
- Pinch of salt and freshly ground black pepper

Directions:

1. Preheat a mini waffle iron and then grease it.
2. For chaffles: In a medium bowl, place all ingredients and with a fork, mix until well combined.
3. Place half of the mixture into preheated waffle iron and cook for about 3-4 minutes or until golden brown.
4. Repeat with the remaining mixture.
5. Serve warm.

Nutrition Info: Per Serving Calories: 173Net Carb: 1.1gFat: 13.7gSaturated Fat: 6.9g Carbohydrates: 2.2gDietary Fiber: 1.1g Sugar: 0.4g Protein: 9.9g

Protein Chaffles

Servings: 1
Cooking Time: 4 Minutes

Ingredients:

- ¼ cup almond milk
- ¼ cup plant-based protein powder
- 2 tbsp almond butter
- 1 tbsp psyllium husk

Directions:

1. Preheat the waffle maker.
2. Combine almond milk, protein powder, psyllium husk and mix thoroughly until the mixture gets the form of a paste.
3. Add in butter, combine well and form round balls
4. Place the ball in the center of preheated waffle maker.
5. Cook for 4 minutes.

6. Remove, top as prefer and enjoy.

Nutrition Info: Calories Per Serving 310 Kcal; Fats: 19 g ; Carbs: 5 g ; Protein: 25 g

Garlic And Spinach Chaffles

Servings: 2

Cooking Time: 5minutes

Ingredients:

- 1 cup egg whites
- 1 tsp. Italian spice
- 2 tsps. coconut flour
- ½ tsp.vanilla
- 1 tsp. baking powder
- 1 tsp. baking soda
- 1 cup mozzarella cheese, grated
- 1/2 tsp. garlic powder
- 1 cup chopped spinach

Directions:

1. Switch on your square waffle maker. Spray with non-stick spray.
2. Beat egg whites with beater, until fluffy and white.
3. Add pumpkin puree, pumpkin pie spice, coconut flour in egg whites and beat again.
4. Stir in the cheese, powder, garlic powder, baking soda, and powder.
5. Sprinkle chopped spinach on a waffle maker
6. Pour the batter in waffle maker over chopped spinach
7. Close the maker and cook for about 4-5 minutes.
8. Remove chaffles from the maker.
9. Serve hot and enjoy!

Nutrition Info: Per Serving: Protein: 52% 88 kcal Fat: 41% 69 kcal Carbohydrates: 7% 12 kcal

Cauliflower Chaffles

Servings: 2

Cooking Time: 5minutes

Ingredients:

- 1 cup egg whites
- 1 cup mozzarella cheese, grated
- ½ cup cauliflower

Directions:

1. Switch on your square waffle maker. Spray with non-stick spray.
2. Mix together all ingredients in a blender.
3. Pour the batter in waffle maker over chopped spinach
4. Close the maker and cook for about 4-5 minutes.
5. Remove chaffles from the maker.
6. Serve hot and enjoy!

Nutrition Info: Per Serving: Protein: 41% 87 kcal Fat: 30% 63 kcal Carbohydrates: 29% 60 kcal

Garlic Powder Chaffles

Servings: 2
Cooking Time: 8 Minutes
Ingredients:

- 1 organic egg, beaten
- ½ cup Monterrey Jack cheese, shredded
- 1 teaspoon coconut flour
- Pinch of garlic powder

Directions:

1. Preheat a mini waffle iron and then grease it.
2. In a bowl, place all the ingredients and beat until well combined.
3. Place half of the mixture into preheated waffle iron and cook for about 3-4 minutes or until golden brown.
4. Repeat with the remaining mixture.
5. Serve warm.

Nutrition Info: Per Serving Calories: 147Net Carb: 1.6gFat: 11.3gSaturated Fat: 6.8g Carbohydrates: 2.1gDietary Fiber: 0.5g Sugar: 0.2g Protein: 9g

Broccoli Chaffles

Servings: 2
Cooking Time: 8 Minutes
Ingredients:

- 1/3 cup raw broccoli, chopped finely
- ¼ cup Cheddar cheese, shredded
- 1 organic egg
- ½ teaspoons garlic powder
- ½ teaspoons dried onion, minced
- Salt and freshly ground black pepper, to taste

Directions:

1. Preheat a mini waffle iron and then grease it.
2. In a medium bowl, place all ingredients and, mix until well combined.
3. Place ¼ of the mixture into preheated waffle iron and cook for about 3-4 minutes or until golden brown.
4. Repeat with the remaining mixture.
5. Serve warm.

Nutrition Info: Per Serving Calories: 96Net Carb: 1.5gFat: 6.9gSaturated Fat: 3.7g Carbohydrates: 2gDietary Fiber: 0.5g Sugar: 0.7g Protein: 6.8g

Parmesan Garlic Chaffle

Servings: 2
Cooking Time: 5 Minutes
Ingredients:

- 1 Tbsp fresh garlic minced
- 2 Tbsp butter
- 1-oz cream cheese, cubed

- 2 Tbsp almond flour
- 1 tsp baking soda
- 2 large eggs
- 1 tsp dried chives
- ½ cup parmesan cheese, shredded
- ¾ cup mozzarella cheese, shredded

Directions:

1. Heat cream cheese and butter in a saucepan over medium-low until melted.
2. Add garlic and cook, stirring, for 2 minutes.
3. Turn on waffle maker to heat and oil it with cooking spray.
4. In a small mixing bowl, whisk together flour and baking soda, then set aside.
5. In a separate bowl, beat eggs for 1 minute 30 seconds on high, then add in cream cheese mixture and beat for 60 seconds more.
6. Add flour mixture, chives, and cheeses to the bowl and stir well.
7. Add ¼ cup batter to waffle maker.
8. Close and cook for 4 minutes, until golden brown.
9. Repeat for remaining batter.
10. Add favorite toppings and serve.

Nutrition Info: Carbs: 5 g ;Fat: 33 g ;Protein: 19 g ;Calories: 385

Spinach & Cauliflower Chaffles

Servings: 2

Cooking Time: 10 Minutes

Ingredients:

- ½ cup frozen chopped spinach, thawed and squeezed
- ½ cup cauliflower, chopped finely
- ½ cup Cheddar cheese, shredded
- ½ cup Mozzarella cheese, shredded
- 1/3 cup Parmesan cheese, , shredded
- 2 organic eggs
- 1 tablespoon butter, melted
- 1 teaspoon garlic powder
- 1 teaspoon onion powder
- Salt and freshly ground black pepper, to taste

Directions:

1. Preheat a waffle iron and then grease it.
2. In a medium bowl, place all ingredients and, mix until well combined.
3. Place half of the mixture into preheated waffle iron and cook for about 4-5 minutes or until golden brown.
4. Repeat with the remaining mixture.
5. Serve warm.

Nutrition Info: Per Serving Calories: 320Net Carb: 4gFat: 24.5gSaturated Fat: 14g Carbohydrates: 5gDietary Fiber: 1g Sugar: 1.9g Protein: 20.8g

Bbq Chicken Chaffles

Servings: 2
Cooking Time: 8 Minutes
Ingredients:
- 1 1/3 cups grass-fed cooked chicken, chopped
- ½ cup Cheddar cheese, shredded
- 1 tablespoon sugar-free BBQ sauce
- 1 organic egg, beaten
- 1 tablespoon almond flour

Directions:
1. Preheat a mini waffle iron and then grease it.
2. In a bowl, place all ingredients and mix until well combined.
3. Place half of the mixture into preheated waffle iron and cook for about 4 minutes or until golden brown.
4. Repeat with the remaining mixture.
5. Serve warm.

Nutrition Info: Per Serving Calories: 320Net Carb: 3.6gFat: 16.3gSaturated Fat: 7.6g Carbohydrates: 4gDietary Fiber: 0.4g Sugar: 2g Protein: 36.9g

Sour Cream Protein Chaffles

Servings: 4
Cooking Time: 16 Minutes
Ingredients:
- 6 organic eggs
- ½ cup sour cream
- ½ cup unsweetened whey protein powder
- 1 teaspoon organic baking powder
- ½ teaspoon salt
- 1 cup Cheddar cheese, shredded

Directions:
1. Preheat a waffle iron and then grease it.
2. In a medium bowl, place all ingredients and mix until well combined.
3. Place ¼ of the mixture into preheated waffle iron and cook for about 3-4 minutes or until golden brown.
4. Repeat with the remaining mixture.
5. Serve warm.

Nutrition Info: Per Serving Calories: 324Net Carb: 3.6gFat: 22.6gSaturated Fat: 11.9g Carbohydrates: 3.6gDietary Fiber: 0g Sugar: 1.3g Protein: 27.3g

Pandan Asian Chaffles

Servings: 2
Cooking Time: 8 Minutes
Ingredients:
- ½ cup cheddar cheese, finely shredded
- 1 egg

- 3 drops of pandan extract
- 1 tbsp almond flour
- 1/3 tsp garlic powder

Directions:

1. Warm up your mini waffle maker.
2. Mix the egg, almond flour, garlic powder with cheese in a small bowl.
3. Add pandan extract to the cheese mixture and mix well.
4. For a crispy crust, add a teaspoon of shredded cheese to the waffle maker and cook for 30 seconds.
5. Then, pour the mixture into the waffle maker and cook for 5 minutes or until crispy.
6. Repeat with remaining batter.
7. Serve with fried chicken wings with bbq sauce and enjoy!
8. Note: more keto stuffing you can find in my air fryer cookbook here:

Nutrition Info: Calories Per Serving 170 Kcal; Fats: 13 g ; Carbs: 2 g ; Protein: 11 g

Cheddar Jalapeño Chaffle

Servings: 2
Cooking Time: 5 Minutes

Ingredients:

- 2 large eggs
- ½ cup shredded mozzarella
- ¼ cup almond flour
- ½ tsp baking powder
- ¼ cup shredded cheddar cheese
- 2 Tbsp diced jalapeños jarred or canned
- For the toppings:
- ½ cooked bacon, chopped
- 2 Tbsp cream cheese
- ¼ jalapeño slices

Directions:

1. Turn on waffle maker to heat and oil it with cooking spray.
2. Mix mozzarella, eggs, baking powder, almond flour, and garlic powder in a bowl.
3. Sprinkle 2 Tbsp cheddar cheese in a thin layer on waffle maker, and ½ jalapeño.
4. Ladle half of the egg mixture on top of the cheese and jalapeños.
5. Cook for 5 minutes, or until done.
6. Repeat for the second chaffle.
7. Top with cream cheese, bacon, and jalapeño slices.

Nutrition Info: Carbs: 5 g ;Fat: 18 g ;Protein: 18 g ;Calories: 307

Cauliflower Chaffle

Servings: 3
Cooking Time: 1 Minutes

Ingredients:

- 2 cup cauliflower, minced
- 2 cup shredded mozzarella cheese

- 2 eggs
- 2 Tbsp almond flour
- ½ tsp paprika
- ½ tsp onion powder
- ½ tsp oregano
- Salt and pepper, to taste
- 3 egg for topping

Directions:

1. Turn on waffle maker to heat and oil it with cooking spray.
2. Combine cauliflower, eggs, cheese, flour, onion powder, paprika, oregano, salt, and pepper.
3. Add 1 cup mixture to waffle maker. Cook for 6 minutes.
4. Remove the first chaffle, repeat with the remaining batter.
5. Fry eggs well.
6. Place a fried egg on top of each chaffle and serve.

Nutrition Info: Carbs: 9 g ;Fat: 19 g ;Protein: 22 g ;Calories: 304

Tuna Chaffles

Servings: 2
Cooking Time: 9 Minutes

Ingredients:

- 1 organic egg, beaten
- ½ cup plus 2 teaspoons Mozzarella cheese, shredded and divided
- 1 (2.6-ounce) can water-packed tuna, drained
- Pinch of salt

Directions:

1. Preheat a mini waffle iron and then grease it.
2. In a bowl, place the egg, ½ cup of Mozzarella cheese, tuna and salt and mix well.
3. Place 1 teaspoon of Mozzarella cheese in the bottom of preheated waffle iron and cook for about 30 seconds.
4. Place the egg mixture over cheese and cook for about 4 minutes or until golden brown.
5. Repeat with the remaining mixture.
6. Serve warm.

Nutrition Info: Per Serving Calories: 94Net Carb: 0.4gFat: 3.7gSaturated Fat: 1.5Carbohydrates: 0.4gDietary Fiber: 0g Sugar: 0.2g Protein: 14.2g

Garlic & Onion Powder Chaffles

Servings: 1
Cooking Time: 5 Minutes

Ingredients:

- 1 organic egg, beaten
- ¼ cup Cheddar cheese, shredded
- 2 tablespoons almond flour
- ½ teaspoon organic baking powder
- ¼ teaspoon garlic powder
- ¼ teaspoon onion powder

- Pinch of salt

Directions:

1. Preheat a waffle iron and then grease it.
2. In a bowl, place all the ingredients and beat until well combined.
3. Place the mixture into preheated waffle iron and cook for about 3-5 minutes or until golden brown.
4. Serve warm.

Nutrition Info: Per Serving Calories: 274Net Carb: 3.3gFat: 21.3gSaturated Fat: 7.8g Carbohydrates: 5gDietary Fiber: 1.7g Sugar: 1.4g Protein: 12.8g

Turkey Chaffle Sandwich

Servings: 6
Cooking Time: 10 Minutes

Ingredients:

- 2 egg whites
- 2 Tbsp almond flour
- 1 Tbsp mayonnaise
- 1 tsp water
- ¼ tsp baking powder
- Pinch of salt
- For the sandwich:
- 2 Tbsp mayonnaise
- 1 slice deli turkey
- 1 slice cheddar cheese
- 1 slice tomato
- 1 leaf green leaf lettuce

Directions:

1. Turn on waffle maker to heat and oil it with cooking spray.
2. Mix all chaffle ingredients in a small bowl.
3. Pour half of the batter into waffle maker and cook for 3-5 minutes.
4. Remove and repeat with remaining batter.
5. Spread mayonnaise on one side of each chaffle. Layer on turkey, tomato and green leaf lettuce.

Nutrition Info: Carbs: 12 g ;Fat: 9 g ;Protein: 11 g ;Calories: 246

Chicken & Veggies Chaffles

Servings: 3
Cooking Time: 15 Minutes

Ingredients:

- 1/3 cup cooked grass-fed chicken, chopped
- 1/3 cup cooked spinach, chopped
- 1/3 cup marinated artichokes, chopped
- 1 organic egg, beaten
- 1/3 cup Mozzarella cheese, shredded
- 1 ounce cream cheese, softened

- ¼ teaspoon garlic powder

Directions:

1. Preheat a mini waffle iron and then grease it.
2. In a medium bowl, place all ingredients and mix until well combined.
3. Place 1/3 of the mixture into preheated waffle iron and cook for about 4-5 minutes or until golden brown.
4. Repeat with the remaining mixture.
5. Serve warm.

Nutrition Info: Per Serving Calories: 95Net Carb: 1.3gFat: 5.8gSaturated Fat: 1.3g Carbohydrates: 2.2gDietary Fiber: 0.9g Sugar: 0.3g Protein: 8.6g

Sausage & Veggies Chaffles

Servings: 4
Cooking Time: 20 Minutes

Ingredients:

- 1/3 cup unsweetened almond milk
- 4 medium organic eggs
- 2 tablespoons gluten-free breakfast sausage, cut into slices
- 2 tablespoons broccoli florets, chopped
- 2 tablespoons bell peppers, seeded and chopped
- 2 tablespoons Mozzarella cheese, shredded

Directions:

1. Preheat a waffle iron and then grease it.
2. In a medium bowl, place the almond milk and eggs and beat well.
3. Place the remaining ingredients and stir to combine well.
4. Place ¼ of the mixture into preheated waffle iron and cook for about 5 minutes or until golden brown.
5. Repeat with the remaining mixture.
6. Serve warm.

Nutrition Info: Per Serving Calories: 132Net Carb: 1.2gFat: 9.2gSaturated Fat: 3.5g Carbohydrates: 1.4gDietary Fiber: 0.2g Sugar: 0.5g Protein: 11.1g

Cheese-free Breakfast Chaffle

Servings: 1
Cooking Time: 12 Minutes

Ingredients:

- 1 egg
- ½ cup almond milk ricotta, finely shredded.
- 1 tbsp almond flour
- 2 tbsp butter

Directions:

1. Mix the egg, almond flour and ricotta in a small bowl.
2. Separate the chaffle batter into two and cook each for 4 minutes.
3. Melt the butter and pour on top of the chaffles.
4. Put them back in the pan and cook on each side for 2 minutes.

5. Remove from the pan and allow them sit for 2 minutes.
6. Enjoy while still crispy.

Nutrition Info: Calories Per Serving 530 Kcal; Fats: 50 g ; Carbs: 3 g ; Protein: 23 g

Chicken Jalapeño Chaffles

Servings: 2
Cooking Time: 10 Minutes

Ingredients:

- ½ cup grass-fed cooked chicken, chopped
- 1 organic egg, beaten
- ¼ cup cheddar cheese, shredded
- 2 tablespoons Parmesan cheese, shredded
- 1 teaspoon cream cheese, softened
- 1 small jalapeño pepper, chopped
- 1/8 teaspoon onion powder
- 1/8 teaspoon garlic powder

Directions:

1. Preheat a mini waffle iron and then grease it.
2. In a medium bowl, put all ingredients and with your hands, mix until well combined.Place half of the mixture into preheated waffle iron and cook for about 4–5 minutes.
3. Repeat with the remaining mixture.
4. Serve warm.

Nutrition Info: Calories 170 Net Carbs 0.9 g Total Fat 9.9 g Saturated Fat 5.2 g Cholesterol 129 mg Sodium 231 mg Total Carbs 1 g Fiber 0.1 g Sugar 0.5 g Protein 18.6 g

Pork Rind Chaffles

Servings: 2
Cooking Time: 10 Minutes

Ingredients:

- 1 organic egg, beaten
- ½ cup ground pork rinds
- 1/3 cup Mozzarella cheese, shredded
- Pinch of salt

Directions:

1. Preheat a mini waffle iron and then grease it.
2. In a bowl, place all the ingredients and beat until well combined.
3. Place half of the mixture into preheated waffle iron and cook for about 3-5 minutes or until golden brown.
4. Repeat with the remaining mixture.
5. Serve warm.

Nutrition Info: Per Serving Calories: 91Net Carb: 0.3gFat: 5.9gSaturated Fat: 2.3g Carbohydrates: 0.3gDietary Fiber: 0g Sugar: 0.2g Protein: 9.2g

Hot Sauce Jalapeño Chaffles

Servings: 2
Cooking Time: 8 Minutes

Ingredients:

- ½ cup plus 2 teaspoons Cheddar cheese, shredded and divided
- 1 organic egg, beaten
- 6 jalapeño pepper slices
- ¼ teaspoon hot sauce
- Pinch of salt

Directions:

1. Preheat a mini waffle iron and then grease it.
2. In a bowl, place ½ cup of cheese and remaining ingredients and mix until well combined.
3. Place about 1 teaspoon of cheese in the bottom of the waffle maker for about 30 seconds before adding the mixture.
4. Place half of the mixture into preheated waffle iron and cook for about 3-4 minutes or until golden brown.
5. Repeat with the remaining cheese and mixture.
6. Serve warm.

Nutrition Info: Per Serving Calories: 153Net Carb: 0.6gFat: 12.2gSaturated Fat: 7g Carbohydrates: 0.7gDietary Fiber: 0.1g Sugar: 0.4g Protein: 10.3g

Chaffle Cuban Sandwich

Servings: 1
Cooking Time: 10 Minutes

Ingredients:

- 1 large egg
- 1 Tbsp almond flour
- 1 Tbsp full-fat Greek yogurt
- ⅛ tsp baking powder
- ¼ cup shredded Swiss cheese
- For the Filling:
- 3 oz roast pork
- 2 oz deli ham
- 1 slice Swiss cheese
- 3-5 sliced pickle chips
- ½ Tbsp Dijon mustard

Directions:

1. Turn on waffle maker to heat and oil it with cooking spray.
2. Beat egg, yogurt, almond flour, and baking powder in a bowl.
3. Sprinkle ¼ Swiss cheese on hot waffle maker. Top with half of the egg mixture, then add ¼ of the cheese on top. Close and cook for 3-5 minutes, until golden brown and crispy.
4. Repeat with remaining batter.
5. Layer pork, ham, and cheese slice in a small microwaveable bowl. Microwave for 50 seconds, until cheese melts.
6. Spread the inside of chaffle with mustard and top with pickles. Invert bowl onto chaffle top so that cheese is touching pickles. Place bottom chaffle onto pork and serve.

Nutrition Info: Carbs: 4 g ;Fat: 46 g ;Protein: 33 g ;Calories: 522

Aioli Chicken Chaffle Sandwich

Servings: 1
Cooking Time: 6 Minutes
Ingredients:
- ¼ cup shredded rotisserie chicken
- 2 Tbsp Kewpie mayo
- ½ tsp lemon juice
- 1 grated garlic clove
- ¼ green onion, chopped
- 1 egg
- ½ cup shredded mozzarella cheese

Directions:
1. Mix lemon juice and mayo in a small bowl.
2. Turn on waffle maker to heat and oil it with cooking spray.
3. Beat egg in a small bowl.
4. Place ⅛ cup of cheese on waffle maker, then spread half of the egg mixture over it and top with ⅛ cup of cheese. Close and cook for 3-4 minutes.
5. Repeat for remaining batter.
6. Place chicken on chaffles and top with sauce. Sprinkle with chopped green onion.

Nutrition Info: Carbs: 3 g ;Fat: 42 g ;Protein: 34 g ;Calories: 545

Scallion Cream Cheese Chaffle

Servings: 2
Cooking Time: 20 Minutes
Ingredients:
- 1 large egg
- ½ cup of shredded mozzarella
- 2 Tbsp cream cheese
- 1 Tbsp everything bagel seasoning
- 1-2 sliced scallions

Directions:
1. Turn on waffle maker to heat and oil it with cooking spray.
2. Beat egg in a small bowl.
3. Add in ½ cup mozzarella.
4. Pour half of the mixture into the waffle maker and cook for 3-4 minutes.
5. Remove chaffle and repeat with remaining mixture.
6. Let them cool, then cover each chaffle with cream cheese, sprinkle with seasoning and scallions.

Nutrition Info: Carbs: 8 g ;Fat: 11 g ;Protein: 5 g ;Calories: 168

FESTIVE CHAFFLE RECIPES

Garlic Chaffle

Servings: 2
Cooking Time: 8 Minutes
Ingredients:

- 1 egg
- ½ cup cheddar cheese, beaten
- 1 teaspoon coconut flour
- Pinch garlic powder

Directions:

1. Plug in your waffle maker.
2. Beat the egg in a bowl.
3. Stir in the rest of the ingredients.
4. Pour half of the batter into your waffle maker.
5. Cook for 4 minutes.
6. Remove the waffle and let sit for 2 minutes.
7. Do the same steps with the remaining batter.

Nutrition Info: Calories 170 Total Fat 14 g Saturated Fat 6 g Cholesterol 121 mg Sodium 220 mg Potassium 165 mg Total Carbohydrate 2 g Dietary Fiber 1 g Protein 10 g Total Sugars 1 g

Almond Butter Chaffle

Servings: 4
Cooking Time: 7–9 Minutes
Ingredients:

- Batter
- 4 eggs
- 4 ounces cream cheese
- 1 teaspoon vanilla extract
- ¼ cup stevia
- ¼ cup almond butter
- 6 tablespoons almond flour
- 1 teaspoon baking powder
- Pinch of salt
- Other
- 2 tablespoons cooking spray to brush the waffle maker
- ¼ cup heavy cream, whipped

Directions:

1. Preheat the waffle maker.
2. Add the eggs and cream cheese to a bowl and stir in the vanilla extract, stevia, almond butter, almond flour, baking powder, and salt. Mix until just combined.
3. Brush the heated waffle maker with cooking spray and add a few tablespoons of the batter.
4. Close the lid and cook for about 7–8 minutes depending on your waffle maker.
5. Serve with whipped cream on top.

Nutrition Info: Per Serving Calories 413, fat 37.8 g, carbs 7.3 g, sugar 1.2 g, Protein 13.5 g, sodium 193 mg

New Year Cinnamon Chaffle With Coconut Cream

Servings: 2
Cooking Time: 5minutes
Ingredients:

- 2 large eggs
- 1/8 cup almond flour
- 1 tsp. cinnamon powder
- 1 tsp. sea salt
- 1/2 tsp. baking soda
- 1 cup shredded mozzarella
- FOR TOPPING
- 2 tbsps. coconut cream
- 1 tbsp. unsweetened chocolate sauce

Directions:

1. Preheat waffle maker according to the manufacturer's directions.
2. Mix together recipe ingredients in a mixing bowl.
3. Add cheese and mix well.
4. Pour about ½ cup mixture into the center of the waffle maker and cook for about 2-3 minutes until golden and crispy.
5. Repeat with the remaining batter.
6. For serving, coat coconut cream over chaffles. Drizzle chocolate sauce over chaffle.
7. Freeze chaffle in the freezer for about10 minutes.
8. Serve on Christmas morning and enjoy!

Nutrition Info: Per Serving: Protein: 39% 100 kcal Fat: 56% 145 kcal Carbohydrates: 5% 13 kcal

Breakfast Peanut Butter Chaffle

Servings: 2
Cooking Time: 15 Minutes
Ingredients:

- 1 egg, lightly beaten
- ½ tsp vanilla
- 1 tbsp Swerve
- 2 tbsp powdered peanut butter
- ½ cup mozzarella cheese, shredded

Directions:

1. Preheat your waffle maker.
2. Add all ingredients into the bowl and mix until well combined.
3. Spray waffle maker with cooking spray.
4. Pour half batter in the hot waffle maker and cook for 5-7 minutes or until golden brown. Repeat with the remaining batter.
5. Serve and enjoy.

Nutrition Info: Calories 80Fat 4.1 g Carbohydrates 2.9 g Sugar 0.6 g Protein 7.4 g Cholesterol 86 mg

Bacon, Egg & Avocado Chaffle Sandwich

Servings: 2
Cooking Time: 10 Minutes

Ingredients:

- Cooking spray
- 4 slices bacon
- 2 eggs
- ½ avocado, mashed
- 4 basic chaffles
- 2 leaves lettuce

Directions:

1. Coat your skillet with cooking spray.
2. Cook the bacon until golden and crisp.
3. Transfer into a paper towel lined plate.
4. Crack the eggs into the same pan and cook until firm.
5. Flip and cook until the yolk is set.
6. Spread the avocado on the chaffle.
7. Top with lettuce, egg and bacon.
8. Top with another chaffle.

Nutrition Info: Calories 372 Total Fat 30.1g Saturated Fat 8.6g Cholesterol 205mg Sodium 943mg Total Carbohydrate 5.4g Dietary Fiber 3.4g Total Sugars 0.6g Protein 20.6g Potassium 524mg

Chicken Quesadilla Chaffle

Servings: 2
Cooking Time: 14 Minutes

Ingredients:

- 1 egg, beaten
- ¼ tsp taco seasoning
- 1/3 cup finely grated cheddar cheese
- 1/3 cup cooked chopped chicken

Directions:

1. Preheat the waffle iron.
2. In a medium bowl, mix the eggs, taco seasoning, and cheddar cheese. Add the chicken and combine well.
3. Open the iron, lightly grease with cooking spray and pour in half of the mixture.
4. Close the iron and cook until brown and crispy, 7 minutes.
5. Remove the chaffle onto a plate and set aside.
6. Make another chaffle using the remaining mixture.
7. Serve afterward.

Nutrition Info: Per Serving Calories 314Fats 20.64gCarbs 5.71gNet Carbs 5.71g Protein 16.74g

Sloppy Joe Chaffle

Servings: 2
Cooking Time: 15 Minutes
Ingredients:

- 1 teaspoon olive oil
- 1 lb. ground beef
- Salt and pepper to taste
- 1 teaspoon onion powder
- 1 teaspoon garlic powder
- 3 tablespoons tomato paste
- 1 tablespoon chili powder
- 1 teaspoon mustard powder
- ½ teaspoon paprika
- ½ cup beef broth
- 1 teaspoon coconut aminos
- 1 teaspoon sweetener
- 4 cornbread chaffles

Directions:

1. Pour the olive oil into a pan over medium high heat.
2. Add the ground beef.
3. Season with salt, pepper and spices.
4. Cook for 5 minutes, stirring occasionally.
5. Stir in the beef broth, coconut aminos and sweetener.
6. Reduce heat and simmer for 10 minutes.
7. Top the cornbread chaffle with the ground beef mixture.
8. Top with another chaffle.

Nutrition Info: Calories 334 Total Fat 12.1g Saturated Fat 4g Cholesterol 135mg Sodium 269mg Potassium 887mgTotal Carbohydrate 6.5g Dietary Fiber 2g Protein 48.2g Total Sugars 2.9g

Lemon And Paprika Chaffles

Servings: 4
Cooking Time: 28 Minutes
Ingredients:

- 1 egg, beaten
- 1 oz cream cheese, softened
- 1/3 cup finely grated mozzarella cheese
- 1 tbsp almond flour
- 1 tsp butter, melted
- 1 tsp maple (sugar-free) syrup
- ½ tsp sweet paprika
- ½ tsp lemon extract

Directions:

1. Preheat the waffle iron.
2. Mix all the ingredients in a medium bowl
3. Open the iron and pour in a quarter of the mixture. Close and cook until crispy, 7 minutes.

4. Remove the chaffle onto a plate and make 3 more with the remaining mixture.
5. Cut each chaffle into wedges, plate, allow cooling and serve.

Nutrition Info: Calories 48Fats 4.22gCarbs 0.6gNet Carbs 0.5g Protein 2g

Pumpkin Spice Chaffles

Servings: 2
Cooking Time: 14 Minutes

Ingredients:

- 1 egg, beaten
- ½ tsp pumpkin pie spice
- ½ cup finely grated mozzarella cheese
- 1 tbsp sugar-free pumpkin puree

Directions:

1. Preheat the waffle iron.
2. In a medium bowl, mix all the ingredients.
3. Open the iron, pour in half of the batter, close, and cook until crispy, 6 to 7 minutes.
4. Remove the chaffle onto a plate and set aside.
5. Make another chaffle with the remaining batter.
6. Allow cooling and serve afterward.

Nutrition Info: Calories 90Fats 6.46gCarbs 1.98gNet Carbs 1.58g Protein 5.94g

Brownie Chaffle

Servings: 4
Cooking Time: 7–9 Minutes

Ingredients:

- Batter
- 4 eggs
- 4 ounces cottage cheese (½ cup)
- 1 teaspoon vanilla extract
- ¼ cup stevia
- ¼ cup melted butter
- ¼ cup almond flour
- 3 tablespoons cocoa powder
- ½ teaspoon baking powder
- Other
- 2 tablespoons butter to brush the waffle maker
- 1 tablespoon cocoa powder for dusting
- ½ cup fresh raspberries for serving

Directions:

1. Preheat the waffle maker.
2. Add the eggs and cottage cheese to a bowl and stir in the vanilla extract, stevia, melted butter, almond flour, cocoa powder, and baking powder. Mix until just combined.
3. Brush the heated waffle maker with butter and add a few tablespoons of the batter.
4. Close the lid and cook for about 7–8 minutes depending on your waffle maker.
5. Serve with dusted cocoa powder and a few raspberries on top.

Nutrition Info: Per Serving Calories 281, fat 23.5 g, carbs 8.1 g, sugar 1.4 g, Protein 12.3 g, sodium 263 mg

Chaffles Icecream Topping

Servings: 2
Cooking Time: 5 Minutes

Ingredients:

- 1/4 cup coconut cream, frozen
- 1 cup coconut flour
- ¼ cup strawberries chunks
- 1 tsp. vanilla extract
- 1 oz. chocolate flakes
- 4 keto chaffles

Directions:

1. Mix together all ingredients in a mixing bowl.
2. Spread mixture between 2 chaffles and freeze in the freezer for 2 hours.
3. Serve chill and enjoy!

Nutrition Info: Per Serving: Protein: 26% 68 kcal Fat: 71% 187 kcal Carbohydrates: 3% 9 kcal

Pizza Flavored Chaffle

Servings: 3
Cooking Time: 12 Minutes

Ingredients:

- 1 egg, beaten
- ½ cup cheddar cheese, shredded
- 2 tablespoons pepperoni, chopped
- 1 tablespoon keto marinara sauce
- 4 tablespoons almond flour
- 1 teaspoon baking powder
- ½ teaspoon dried Italian seasoning
- Parmesan cheese, grated

Directions:

1. Preheat your waffle maker.
2. In a bowl, mix the egg, cheddar cheese, pepperoni, marinara sauce, almond flour, baking powder and Italian seasoning.
3. Add the mixture to the waffle maker.
4. Close the device and cook for 4 minutes.
5. Open it and transfer chaffle to a plate.
6. Let cool for 2 minutes.
7. Repeat the steps with the remaining batter.
8. Top with the grated Parmesan and serve.

Nutrition Info: Calories 179 Total Fat 14.3g Saturated Fat 7.5g Cholesterol 118mg Sodium 300mg Potassium 326mg Total Carbohydrate 1.8g Dietary Fiber 0.1g Protein 11.1g Total Sugars 0.4g

Sweet Vanilla Chocolate Chaffle

Servings: 1
Cooking Time: 10 Minutes
Ingredients:

- 1 egg, lightly beaten
- 1/4 tsp cinnamon
- 1/2 tsp vanilla
- 1 tbsp Swerve
- 2 tsp unsweetened cocoa powder
- 1 tbsp coconut flour
- 2 oz cream cheese, softened

Directions:

1. Add all ingredients into the small bowl and mix until well combined.
2. Spray waffle maker with cooking spray.
3. Pour batter in the hot waffle maker and cook until golden brown.
4. Serve and enjoy.

Nutrition Info: Calories 312Fat 25.4 g Carbohydrates 11.5 g Sugar 0.8 g Protein 11.6 g Cholesterol 226 mg

Mini Keto Pizza

Servings: 2
Cooking Time: 15 Minutes
Ingredients:

- 1 egg
- ½ cup mozzarella cheese, shredded
- ¼ teaspoon basil
- ¼ teaspoon garlic powder
- 1 tablespoon almond flour
- ½ teaspoon baking powder
- 2 tablespoons reduced-carb pasta sauce
- 2 tablespoons mozzarella cheese

Directions:

1. Preheat your waffle maker.
2. In a bowl, beat the egg.
3. Stir in the ½ cup mozzarella cheese, basil, garlic powder, almond flour and baking powder.
4. Add half of the mixture to your waffle maker.
5. Cook for 4 minutes.
6. Transfer to a baking sheet.
7. Cook the second mini pizza.
8. While both pizzas are on the baking sheet, spread the pasta sauce on top.
9. Sprinkle the cheese on top.
10. Bake in the oven until the cheese has melted.

Nutrition Info: Calories 195 Total Fat 14 g Saturated Fat 6 g Cholesterol 116 mg Sodium 301 mg Potassium 178 mg Total Carbohydrate 4 g Dietary Fiber 1 g Protein 13 g Total Sugars 1 g

Chaffle With Cream Topping

Servings: 4
Cooking Time: 5minutes
Ingredients:

- 1 cup egg whites
- ½ tsp.vanilla
- 1 tsp. baking powder
- 1 cup mozzarella cheese, grated
- TOPPING
- ½ cup frozen heavy cream
- Cherries

Directions:

1. Switch on your square waffle maker. Spray with non-stick spray.
2. Beat egg whites with beater, until fluffy and white.
3. Stir in the cheese, baking powder and vanilla.
4. Pour ½ of the batter in a waffle maker.
5. Close the maker and cook for about 3 minutes.
6. Repeat with the remaining batter.
7. Remove chaffles from the maker.
8. Serve with heavy cream and cherries on top and enjoy!

Nutrition Info: Per Serving: Protein: 38% 133 kcal Fat: 57% 201 kcal Carbohydrates: 5% 18 kcal

Chaffles And Ice-cream Platter

Servings: 2
Cooking Time: 5 minutes
Ingredients:

- 2 keto brownie chaffles
- 2 scoop vanilla keto ice cream
- 8 oz. strawberries, sliced
- keto chocolate sauce

Directions:

1. Arrange chaffles, ice-cream, strawberries slice in serving plate.
2. Drizzle chocolate sauce on top.
3. Serve and enjoy!

Nutrition Info: Per Serving: Protein: 26% 48 kcal Fat: 68% 128 kcal Carbohydrates: 6% 11 kcal

Bacon, Olives & Cheddar Chaffle

Servings: 2
Cooking Time: 8 Minutes
Ingredients:

- 1 egg
- ½ cup cheddar cheese, shredded
- 1 tablespoon black olives, chopped
- 1 tablespoon bacon bits

Directions:

1. Plug in your waffle maker.
2. In a bowl, beat the egg and stir in the cheese.
3. Add the black olives and bacon bits.
4. Mix well.
5. Add half of the mixture into the waffle maker.
6. Cover and cook for 4 minutes.
7. Open and transfer to a plate.
8. Let cool for 2 minutes.
9. Cook the other chaffle using the remaining batter.

Nutrition Info: Calories 202 Total Fat 16g Saturated Fat 8g Cholesterol 122mg Sodium 462mg Potassium 111mg Total Carbohydrate 0.9g Dietary Fiber 0.1g Protein 13.4g Total Sugars 0.3g

Blueberry Chaffle

Servings: 2
Cooking Time: 8 Minutes
Ingredients:

- 1 egg, beaten
- ½ cup mozzarella cheese, shredded
- 1 teaspoon baking powder
- 2 tablespoons almond flour
- 2 teaspoons sweetener
- ¼ cup blueberries, chopped

Directions:

1. Combine all the ingredients in a bowl. Mix well.
2. Turn on the waffle maker.
3. Pour half of the mixture into the cooking device.
4. Close it and cook for 4 minutes.
5. Open the waffle maker and transfer to a plate.
6. Let cool for 2 minutes.
7. Add the remaining mixture to the waffle maker and repeat the steps.

Nutrition Info: Calories 175 Total Fat 4.3g Saturated Fat 1.5g Cholesterol 86mg Sodium 76mg Potassium 296mg Total Carbohydrate 6.6g Dietary Fiber 1.7g Protein 5.3g Total Sugars 2g

Oreo Cookies Chaffles

Servings: 3
Cooking Time: 5 minutes
Ingredients:

- 1 egg
- 2 tbsps. almond flour
- 1 tbsp. peanut butter
- 1/2 tsp. baking powder
- 1 tsp. stevia

- 2 tbsps. cream cheese
- 2 tbsps. black cocoa powder
- 1 tbsp. mayonnaise
- 2 tbsps. chocolate chips

Directions:

1. In a small bowl, beat an egg with an electric beater.
2. Add the remaining ingredients and mix well until the batter is smooth and fluffy.
3. Divide the batter into 3 portions.
4. Pour the batter in a round greased waffle maker.
5. Cook Oreo chaffle cookies for about 2-3 minutes until cooked.
6. Drizzle coconut flour on top.
7. Serve and enjoy!

Nutrition Info: Per Serving: Protein: 22% 29 kcal Fat: 72% 96 kcal Carbohydrates: 7% 9 kcal

Cinnamon And Vanilla Chaffle

Servings: 4
Cooking Time: 7–9 Minutes

Ingredients:

- Batter
- 4 eggs
- 4 ounces sour cream
- 1 teaspoon vanilla extract
- 1 teaspoon cinnamon
- ¼ cup stevia
- 5 tablespoons coconut flour
- Other
- 2 tablespoons coconut oil to brush the waffle maker
- ½ teaspoon cinnamon for garnishing the chaffles

Directions:

1. Preheat the waffle maker.
2. Add the eggs and sour cream to a bowl and stir with a wire whisk until just combined.
3. Add the vanilla extract, cinnamon, and stevia and mix until combined.
4. Stir in the coconut flour and stir until combined.
5. Brush the heated waffle maker with coconut oil and add a few tablespoons of the batter.
6. Close the lid and cook for about 7–8 minutes depending on your waffle maker.
7. Serve and enjoy.

Nutrition Info: Per Serving Calories 224, fat 18.1 g, carbs 8.4 g, sugar 0.5 g, Protein 7.7 g, sodium 77 mg

Crunchy Coconut Chaffles Cake

Servings: 4
Cooking Time: 15 Minutes

Ingredients:

- 4 large eggs
- 1 cup shredded cheese

- 2 tbsps. coconut cream
- 2 tbsps. coconut flour.
- 1 tsp. stevia
- TOPPING
- 1 cup heavy cream
- 8 oz. raspberries
- 4 oz. blueberries
- 2 oz. cherries

Directions:

1. Make 4 thin round chaffles with the chaffle ingredients. Once chaffles are cooked, set in layers ona plate.
2. Spread heavy cream in each layer.
3. Top with raspberries then blueberries and cherries.
4. Serve and enjoy!

Nutrition Info: Per Serving: Protein: 21% 67 kcal Fat: 72% 230 kcal Carbohydrates: 7% 21 kcal

Herby Chaffle Snacks

Servings: 4
Cooking Time: 28 Minutes

Ingredients:

- 1 egg, beaten
- ½ cup finely grated Monterey Jack cheese
- ¼ cup finely grated Parmesan cheese
- ½ tsp dried mixed herbs

Directions:

1. Preheat the waffle iron.
2. Mix all the ingredients in a medium bowl
3. Open the iron and pour in a quarter of the mixture. Close and cook until crispy, 7 minutes.
4. Remove the chaffle onto a plate and make 3 more with the rest of the ingredients.
5. Cut each chaffle into wedges and plate.
6. Allow cooling and serve.

Nutrition Info: Calories 96Fats 6.29gCarbs 2.19gNet Carbs 2.19g Protein 7.42g

Quick & Easy Blueberry Chaffle

Servings: 2
Cooking Time: 15 Minutes

Ingredients:

- 1 egg, lightly beaten
- 1/4 cup blueberries
- 1/2 tsp vanilla
- 1 oz cream cheese
- 1/4 tsp baking powder, gluten-free
- 4 tsp Swerve
- 1 tbsp coconut flour

Directions:

1. Preheat your waffle maker.
2. In a small bowl, mix coconut flour, baking powder, and Swerve until well combined.
3. Add vanilla, cream cheese, egg, and vanilla and whisk until combined.
4. Spray waffle maker with cooking spray.
5. Pour half batter in the hot waffle maker and top with 4-5 blueberries and cook for 4-5 minutes until golden brown. Repeat with the remaining batter.
6. Serve and enjoy.

Nutrition Info: Calories 135Fat 8.2 g Carbohydrates 11 g Sugar 2.6 g Protein 5 g Cholesterol 97 mg

Choco Waffle With Cream Cheese

Servings: 2
Cooking Time: 8 Minutes

Ingredients:

- Choco Chaffle
- 2 tablespoons cocoa powder
- 1 tablespoon almond flour
- ¼ teaspoon baking powder
- 2 tablespoons sweetener
- 1 egg, beaten
- ½ teaspoon vanilla extract
- 1 tablespoon heavy whipping cream
- Frosting
- 2 tablespoons cream cheese
- 2 teaspoons confectioner's sugar (swerve)
- 1/8 teaspoon vanilla extract
- 1 teaspoon heavy cream

Directions:

1. Combine all the choco chaffle ingredients in a large bowl, adding the wet ingredients last.
2. Mix well.
3. Plug in your waffle maker.
4. Pour half of the mixture into the device.
5. Close and cook for 4 minutes.
6. Cook the other waffle.
7. While waiting, make your frosting by adding cream cheese to a heat proof bowl.
8. Place in the microwave.
9. Microwave for 8 seconds.
10. Use a mixer to blend the cream cheese with the rest of the frosting ingredients.
11. Process until fluffy.
12. Spread the frosting on top of the chaffle.
13. Put another chaffle on top.
14. Pipe the rest of the frosting on top of the chaffle.
15. Slice and serve.

Nutrition Info: Calories 151 Total Fat 13 g Saturated Fat 6 g Cholesterol 111 mg Sodium 83 mg Potassium 190 mg Total Carbohydrate 5 g Dietary Fiber 2 g Protein 6 g Total Sugars 1 g

Walnuts Lowcarb Chaffles

Servings: 2
Cooking Time:5 minutes

Ingredients:

- 2 tbsps. cream cheese
- ½ tsp almonds flour
- ¼ tsp. baking powder
- 1 large egg
- ¼ cup chopped walnuts
- Pinch of stevia extract powder

Directions:

1. Preheat your waffle maker.
2. Spray waffle maker with cooking spray.
3. In a bowl, add cream cheese, almond flour, baking powder, egg, walnuts, and stevia.
4. Mix all ingredients,
5. Spoon walnut batter in the waffle maker and cook for about 2-3 minutes.
6. Let chaffles cool at room temperature before serving.

Nutrition Info: Per Serving: Protein: 12% 11 kcal Fat: 80% 76 kcal Carbohydrates: 8% 8 kcal

Choco Chip Lemon Chaffle

Servings: 2
Cooking Time: 15 Minutes

Ingredients:

- 2 eggs, lightly beaten
- 1 tbsp unsweetened chocolate chips
- 2 tsp Swerve
- 1/2 tsp vanilla
- 1/2 tsp lemon extract
- 1/2 cup mozzarella cheese, shredded
- 2 tsp almond flour

Directions:

1. Preheat your waffle maker.
2. In a bowl, whisk eggs, Swerve, vanilla, lemon extract, cheese, and almond flour.
3. Add chocolate chips and stir well.
4. Spray waffle maker with cooking spray.
5. Pour 1/2 of the batter in the hot waffle maker and cook for 4-5 minutes or until golden brown. Repeat with the remaining batter.
6. Serve and enjoy.

Nutrition Info: Calories 157Fat 10.8 g Carbohydrates 5.4 g Sugar 0.7 g Protein 9 g Cholesterol 167 mg

OTHER DELICIOUS KETO CHAFFLE RECIPES

Shrimp Avocado Chaffle Sandwich

Servings: 4
Cooking Time: 32 Minutes
Ingredients:

- 2 cups shredded mozzarella cheese
- 4 large eggs
- ½ tsp curry powder
- ½ tsp oregano
- Shrimp Sandwich Filling:
- 1-pound raw shrimp (peeled and deveined)
- 1 large avocado (diced)
- 4 slices cooked bacon
- 2 tbsp sour cream
- ½ tsp paprika
- 1 tsp Cajun seasoning
- 1 tbsp olive oil
- ¼ cup onion (finely chopped)
- 1 red bell pepper (diced)

Directions:

1. Plug the waffle maker to preheat it and spray it with a non-stick cooking spray.
2. Break the eggs into a mixing bowl and beat. Add the cheese, oregano and curry. Mix until the ingredients are well combined.
3. Pour an appropriate amount of the batter into the waffle maker and spread out the batter to the edges to cover all the holes on the waffle maker. This should make 8 mini waffles.
4. Close the waffle maker and cook for about 4 minutes or according to your waffle maker's settings.
5. After the cooking cycle, use a silicone or plastic utensil to remove the chaffle from the waffle maker.
6. Repeat step 3 to 5 until you have cooked all the batter into chaffles.
7. Heat up the olive oil in a large skillet over medium to high heat.
8. Add the shrimp and cook until the shrimp is pink and tender.
9. Remove the skillet from heat and use a slotted spoon to transfer the shrimp to a paper towel lined plate to drain for a few minutes.
10. Put the shrimp in a mixing bowl. Add paprika and Cajun seasoning. Toss until the shrimps are all coated with seasoning.
11. To assemble the sandwich, place one chaffle on a flat surface and spread some sour cream over it. Layer some shrimp, onion, avocado, diced pepper and one slice of bacon over it. Cover with another chaffle.
12. Repeat step 10 until you have assembled all the ingredients into sandwiches.
13. Serve and enjoy.

Nutrition Info: Per Serving Fat 32.1g 41% Carbohydrate 10.8g 4% Sugars 2.5g Protein 44.8g

Broccoli And Cheese Chaffle

Servings: 1

Cooking Time: 15 Minutes

Ingredients:

- 1/3 cup broccoli (finely chopped)
- ½ tsp oregano
- 1/8 tsp salt or to taste
- 1/8 tsp ground black pepper or to taste'
- ½ tsp garlic powder
- ½ tsp onion powder
- 1 egg (beaten)
- 4 tbsp shredded cheddar cheese

Directions:

1. Plug the waffle maker to preheat it and spray it with a non-stick cooking spray.
2. In a mixing bowl, combine the cheese, oregano, pepper, garlic, salt and onion. Add the egg and mix until the ingredients are well combined.
3. Fold in the chopped broccoli.
4. Pour an appropriate amount of the batter into your waffle maker and spread out the batter to the edges to cover all the holes on the waffle maker.
5. Close the waffle maker and cook for about 6-8 until the chaffle is browned. Cook time may vary in some waffle makers.
6. After the cooking cycle, use a silicone or plastic utensil to remove the chaffle from the waffle maker.
7. Repeat step 4 to 6 until you have cooked all the batter into chaffles.
8. Serve and top with sour cream as desired.

Nutrition Info: Per Serving Fat 13.9g 18% Carbohydrate 5.2g 2% Sugars 1.8g Protein 13.9g

Choco Peanut Butter Chaffle

Servings: 2

Cooking Time: 10 Minutes

Ingredients:

- Filling:
- 3 tbsp all-natural peanut butter
- 2 tsp swerve sweetener
- 1 tsp vanilla extract
- 2 tbsp heavy cream
- Chaffle:
- ¼ tsp baking powder
- 1 tbsp unsweetened cocoa powder
- 4 tsp almond flour
- ½ tsp vanilla extract
- 1 tbsp granulated swerve sweetener
- 1 large egg (beaten)
- 1 tbsp heavy cream

Directions:

1. For the chaffle:
2. Plug the waffle maker and preheat it. Spray it with a non-stick spray.
3. In a large mixing bowl, combine the almond flour, cocoa powder, baking powder and swerve.

4. Add the egg, vanilla extract and heavy cream. Mix until the ingredients are well combined and you form a smooth batter.
5. Pour some of the batter into the preheated waffle maker. Spread out the batter to the edges of the waffle maker to cover all the holes on the waffle iron.
6. Close the lid of the waffle iron and bake for about 5 minutes or according to waffle maker's settings.
7. After the baking cycle, use a plastic or silicone utensil to remove the chaffle from the waffle maker.
8. Repeat step 4 to 6 until you have cooked all the batter into chaffles.
9. Transfer the chaffles to a wire rack and let the chaffles cool completely.
10. For the filling:
11. Combine the vanilla, swerve, heavy cream and peanut butter in a bowl. Mix until the ingredients are well combined.
12. Spread the peanut butter frosting over the chaffles and serve.
13. Enjoy.

Nutrition Info: Per Serving Fat 43.2g 55% Carbohydrate 32g12% Sugars 9g Protein 19g

Avocado Chaffles

Servings: 2
Cooking Time: 5 Minutes

Ingredients:

- 1 large egg
- 1/2 cup finely shredded mozzarella
- 1/8 cup avocado mash
- 1 tbsp. coconut cream
- TOPPING
- 2 oz. smoked salmon
- 1 Avocado thinly sliced

Directions:

1. Switch on your square waffle maker and grease with cooking spray.
2. Beat egg in a mixing bowl with a fork.
3. Add the cheese, avocado mash and coconut cream to the egg and mix well.
4. Pour chaffle mixture in thepreheated waffle maker and cook for about 2-3 minutes.
5. Once chaffles are cooked, carefully remove from the maker.
6. Serve with an avocado slice and smoked salmon.
7. Drizzle ground pepper on top.
8. Enjoy!

Nutrition Info: Per Serving: Protein: 23% 90 kcal Fat: 67% 266 kcal Carbohydrates: 11% 42 kcal

Keto Avocado Chaffle Toast

Servings: 1
Cooking Time: 8 Minutes

Ingredients:

- Avocado Topping:

- 1 tbsp butter
- 1 green bell pepper (finely chopped)
- ½ cup feta cheese
- ½ avocado
- 1 tsp lemon juice
- ¼ tsp nutmeg
- ¼ tsp onion powder
- ½ tsp ground black pepper or to taste
- Chaffle:
- ½ mozzarella cheese
- 1 egg (beaten)
- 1 tbsp Almond flour
- 1 tsp cinnamon
- ½ tsp baking soda

Directions:

1. Plug the waffle maker tom preheat it and spray it with a non-stick spray.
2. In a mixing bowl, combine the mozzarella, almond flour, baking soda and cinnamon. Add the egg and mix until the ingredients are well combined and you form a smooth batter.
3. Fill the waffle maker with appropriate amount of the batter and spread the batter to the edges of the waffle maker to cover all the holes on the waffle iron.
4. Close the lid of the waffle maker and cook for about 3 to 4 minutes or according to waffle maker's settings.
5. Meanwhile, dice the avocado into a bowl and mash until smooth. Add the bell pepper, nutmeg, onion powder, ground pepper and lemon juice. Mix until well combined.
6. After the baking cycle, remove the chaffle the waffle maker with a silicone or plastic utensil.
7. Repeat step 3, 4 and 6 until you have cooked all the batter into chaffles.
8. Brush the butter over the chaffles. Spread the avocado mixture over the chaffles. Top with shredded feta cheese.
9. Serve and enjoy.

Nutrition Info: Per Serving Fat 68.6g 88% Carbohydrate 31g 11% Sugars 11.5g Protein 29.8g

Tuna Salad Chaffles

Servings: 2
Cooking Time: 8 Minutes

Ingredients:

- Tuna Sandwich:
- 1 can water packed tuna (drained)
- 1 small sweet onion (chopped)
- 1 green bell pepper (finely chopped)
- 1 small carrot (peeled and chopped)
- 2 tbsp mayonnaise
- ½ tsp paprika
- ¼ tsp ground black pepper or to taste
- ¼ tsp salt or to taste
- 1 celery stalk (chopped)
- 1 tbsp freshly chopped parsley

- Chaffle:
- 2 eggs (beaten)
- 4 tbsp almond flour
- 1 cup shredded mozzarella cheese
- ¾ tsp baking powder
- ½ tsp garlic powder

Directions:

1. Plug the waffle maker to preheat it and spray the it with a non-stick cooking spray.
2. In a mixing bowl, combine the almond flour, baking powder, garlic powder and mozzarella. Add the eggs and mix until the ingredients are well combined.
3. Fill the waffle maker with an appropriate amount of the batter and spread the batter to the edges to cover all the holes on the waffle maker.
4. Close the waffle maker and cook for about 4 minutes or according to waffle maker's settings.
5. After the cooking cycle, use a silicone or plastic utensil to remove the chaffle from the waffle maker.
6. Repeat step 3 to 5 until you have cooked all the batter into chaffles.
7. In a mixing bowl, combine the tuna, celery, pepper, onion, salt, paprika, carrot, onion and green pepper. Add the mayonnaise and toss until the ingredients are well combined.
8. Place one of the chaffle of a flat surface and spoon ½ of the tuna salad into it. Top with fresh parsley. Cover it with another chaffle and press.
9. Repeat step 8 to make the second sandwich.
10. Serve and enjoy.

Nutrition Info: Per Serving Fat 26.3g 34% Carbohydrate 19.6g 7% Sugars 7.7g Protein 37.8g

Keto Pizza Chaffle

Servings: 2
Cooking Time: 15 Minutes

Ingredients:

- Pizza Filing:
- 1/3 cups pepperoni slices
- 1 tbsp marinara sauce
- ½ cup shredded mozzarella cheese
- 1 onion (finely chopped)
- 1 small green bell pepper (finely chopped)
- Chaffle:
- 1 egg (beaten)
- A pinch of Italian seasoning
- A pinch of salt
- ½ cup mozzarella cheese
- ¼ tsp baking powder
- ½ tsp dried basil
- A pinch of garlic powder
- 1 tbsp + 1 tsp almond flour

Directions:

1. Preheat the oven to 400°F and line a baking sheet with parchment paper.
2. Plug the waffle maker and preheat it. Spray it with a nonstick spray.

3. For the chaffle: In a mixing bowl, combine the baking powder, almond flour, garlic powder, Italian seasoning, basil, mozzarella cheese and salt. Add the egg and mix until the ingredients are well combined.
4. Fill the waffle maker with appropriate amount of the batter and spread the batter to the edges of the waffle maker to cover all the holes on the waffle maker.
5. Close the lid of the waffle maker and cook for about 5 minutes or according to waffle maker's settings.
6. After the baking cycle, remove the chaffle from waffle maker with a silicone or plastic utensil.
7. Repeat step 4 to 6 until you have cooked all the batter into chaffles.
8. Top each of the chaffles with the marinara sauce, sprinkle the finely chopped onions and pepper over the chaffles.
9. Top with shredded mozzarella cheese and layer the pepperoni slices on the cheese topping.
10. Gently place the chaffles on the lined baking sheet. Place the baking sheet in the oven and bake for about 5 minutes. Afterwards, broil for about 1 minute.
11. Remove the pizza chaffles from the oven and let them cook for a few minutes.
12. Serve warm and enjoy.

Nutrition Info: Per Serving Fat 23.2g 30% Carbohydrate 14.9g 5% Sugars 6.8g Protein 16.8g

Savory Chaffle Stick

Servings: 16
Cooking Time: 25 Minutes

Ingredients:

- 6 eggs
- 2 cups shredded mozzarella cheese
- A pinch of salt
- ½ tsp ground black pepper or to taste
- ½ tsp baking powder
- 4 tbsp coconut flour
- 1 tsp onion powder
- 1 tsp garlic powder
- 1 tsp oregano
- ¼ tsp Italian seasoning
- 1 tbsp olive oil
- 1 tbsp melted butter

Directions:

1. Plug the waffle maker to preheat it and spray it with a non-stick cooking spray.
2. Break 4 of the eggs into a mixing bowl and beat. Add the coconut flour, baking powder, salt, cheese and Italian seasoning. Combine until the ingredients are well combined. Add more flour if the mixture is too thick.
3. Pour an appropriate amount of the batter into the waffle maker and spread out the batter to cover all the holes on the waffle maker.
4. Cover the waffle maker and cook for about 7 minutes or according to your waffle maker's settings. Make sure the chaffle is browned.
5. After the cooking cycle, use a plastic or silicone utensil to remove the chaffle form the waffle maker.
6. Repeat step 3 to 5 until you have cooked all the batter into chaffles.
7. Cut the chaffles into sticks. Each mini chaffle should make about 4 sticks.

8. Preheat the oven to 350°F. Line a baking sheet with parchment paper and grease it with the melted butter.
9. Break the remaining two eggs into another mixing bowl and beat.
10. In another mixing bowl, combine the oregano, pepper, garlic and onion.
11. Dip one chaffle stick into the egg. Bring it out and hold it for a few seconds to allow excess liquid to drip off.
12. Dip the wet chaffle stick into the seasoning mixture and make sure it is coated with seasoning. Drop it on the baking sheet.
13. Repeat step 11 and 12 until all the chaffle sticks are coated.
14. Arrange the chaffle sticks into the baking sheet in a single layer.
15. Place the baking sheet in the oven and bake for 10 minutes.
16. Remove the baking sheet from the oven, brush the oil over the sticks and flip them.
17. Return it to the oven and bake for an additional 6 minutes or until the stick are golden brown.
18. Remove the sticks from the oven and let them cool for a few minutes.
19. Serve and enjoy.

Nutrition Info: Per Serving Fat 4.1g 5% Carbohydrate 2g 1% Sugars 0.2g Protein 3.4g

CPSIA information can be obtained
at www.ICGtesting.com
Printed in the USA
BVHW060104190221
600496BV00011B/858

9 781801 662123